My Now for the
Future Woman

My Now for the
Future Woman

Moovin4ward Publishing
Huntsville, Alabama

Copyright 2016 Moovin4ward Publishing

Library of Congress Control Number: 2016910640

ISBN: Paperback   978-0-9910227-79

Printed in the United States of America

All rights reserved. No part of this publication may be reproduced, stored in a retrieval system or transmitted in any form or by any means, electronic, mechanical, photocopying, recording or otherwise, without the written permission of the publisher.

Publisher:
    Moovin4ward Publishing
    A Division of Moovin4ward Presentations LLC
    www.Moovin4ward.com

Contents

Part 1: My Vision 7

    Know Yourself… First 9
    The Inner Compass 17
    A Woman's Work is Her Worth 25
    Seeing is Believing 35

Part 2: My Plan 43

    Accepting the STAR Power Within 45
    Kryptonite 53
    Protecting the Future You… Now 61
    Boss Lady Basics 69
    Your Living Herstory and Legacy 81

Part 3: My Now 93

    Why Now and Not Then? 95
    Not Tomorrow 105
    Can't Stop Now, Destiny is Calling 115
    @MyPrincess #URRoyalty 129
    Journey 137

My Now…

...for the Future Woman

Part 1: My Vision

My Now...

Pamela Glowski

Pamela Glowski resides in Northeast Ohio and is currently a CTA Certified Life and Human Capital Business Coach as well as the owner of Serene Insights, LLC.

Pamela's purpose is to assist all of her clients, as their "Change Coach", while they work from transition to transformation, and achieve new found success and results. After solidifying her own success, she chose once again to follow her entrepreneurial spirit and launched Serene Insights in late January of 2014.

Pamela's first entrepreneurial venture came within the travel industry in 2005. She had developed proven strategies and had earned a position as a trainer and featured speaker in several Direct Sales Events including webinars, conference calls and live appearances.

Pamela is a CTA Certified Coach in both Life/Business Coaching as well as Human Capital Coaching. Her years of education and experience in working with all types of individuals and companies has allowed her to gain insights that enable her to create and use powerful coaching techniques, accountability steps and true compassion to allow her clients to "Create The Life You Can't Wait To Live"!!

If you would like to learn more about Serene Insights and Coaching with Pamela contact her directly at Pamela@sereneinsightscoaching.com
You can also visit her website at www.sereneinsightscoaching.com

...for the *Future Woman*

Know Yourself... First

Pamela Glowski

"If I only would have known then, what I know now!"

Later this year, I will celebrate my 50th Birthday, and it seems everyone asks, "How do you feel about turning 50?" "If I only would have known then, what I know now!" seems to be my usual answer.

In some ways, I'm overjoyed at the thought of being 50, and in other ways it seems a bit melancholy. Melancholy only because I just can't believe how fast the time has gone. Everyone young hears "time flies" from those who are older, and the statement is usually met with instant disregard from the younger person. It did for me too! When I was 20, I thought that 50 was forever away, and that 30 years was more than enough time to work through my list of dreams and goals. Now that I am facing the mid-mark to my life, I realize I have so much more work that I want to accomplish, lands I have yet to see, and differences I want to make in the world.

I celebrate the thought of my birthday milestone because as I reflect on my first 49 years, I realize how much I've grown. I realize how much I've experienced, and learned, that will allow me to continue my journey with great vigor and enthusiasm.

Of course through the years, my dreams and goals have changed. As I have evolved, based on what I have learned and experienced, my goals and desires for my life have changed too. I think that is a good thing; nothing lasts forever and I can only think of a few things that I'd never want to change. As I have had the opportunity to expand my knowledge, and learn through mentorship and experiences, my eyes have been opened to a bigger world with bigger possibilities; the changes were inevitable. When I was 32 years old, I had my life changing realization that shaped much of my personal evolution. It stems from a simple concept. That concept is KNOW YOURSELF and SEIZE YOUR POWER…FIRST! Then make choices that allow you to create your life by design, rather than by default, or at the will of others. Since that epiphany, I have consciously made it a point to constantly build my relationship with myself and it has led to much better success.

We've all heard the analogy regarding loss of oxygen during a flight. There is always huge emphasis on putting the air bag on yourself before you assist others. It's the same in life. You have to take care of yourself first before you can possibly live at a high level of personal fulfillment, help others, have a healthy relationship or accomplish any collaborative goal.

In my pursuit of that higher understanding of myself, I learned that it takes time and effort. It takes reflection and forecasting. Stopping oneself can be very difficult in the busy world we live in, but it has to be done. Taking an inventory of our feelings, our views, what is non-negotiable and what is open to compromise, is a critical step in predicting any intended outcome. It's also important to continue to stay conscious as we move toward the goal so we are able to make corrections along the way. I have taken the time to get to KNOW myself, my feelings, what my purpose is, what my values are. We all must do it!

When I was younger, I didn't take that time at first. In my generation, that wasn't really encouraged. It was more about obedience and listening to either parents, teachers, religious leaders or others, to "fit a mold". It wasn't about thinking for myself. Thankfully, we've come a long way, baby! Parenting is different now. Women have more of a voice than they have ever had before. Youth has a stronger voice and more choices, than it has ever had before.

Because of the outside influences, I found myself on paths that other people wanted for me. I found myself trying to make others happy. I didn't want to disappoint anyone or do the wrong thing. I found myself playing small because I didn't trust myself enough to step into my own personal power.

My Now…

Now with all of that being said, I wish I would have learned these techniques at a much younger age. I would hope that we will encourage all of our children, not only our daughters to begin this at age 12. Part of the KNOWING OURSELVES AND SEIZING OUR POWER is letting others in our lives do the same. That means as mothers we need to allow our children to choose paths for themselves without injecting our own agendas into their decision making process. WE may not always like it or agree, but if we expect ourselves and our children to follow our passions and live healthy, full lives, we must give each other the mutual respect to KNOW OURSELVES AND SEIZE OUR POWER…FIRST.

By not checking with myself first to make sure the goals were what I wanted too, I often times found myself frustrated, sad, unfulfilled, unsuccessful and not really functioning to the best of my ability. You truly cannot live for anyone else and expect to thrive and be at peace.

Now, I embrace who I really am, and know that every choice that I make is either going to support my effort to leading a successful life or it's not. When I am in my own authenticity, the more that I seem to be able to do and the happier I am doing it. Usually the people around me are a lot happier as well. Whether that's work, hobbies, or relationships, when I am being my true self, it just all seems to flow. Just by me being who I truly am.

...for the Future Woman

I have the confidence to stand in my own shoes, choosing my paths based on what I know is going to lead me to my own success. Confidence is what leads to SEIZING YOUR POWER. Confidence NEVER means taking advantage of anyone or doing things that are immoral, dishonest or demeaning to anyone else. Confidence is not selfish. In fact, you are less selfish when you come from a place of power rather than self-centeredness. When you are confident in yourself and your abilities you can see beyond your own situation and consider the consequences of your actions; how they affect everyone involved in your life. Confidence gives you the ability to make choices BEFORE you commit to the idea, rather than blindly, or by the influence of others, agree to jobs, relationships, hobbies, or special interest groups. You know what a "right fit" is for you, and what isn't, and you can stand confidently in that choice.

Confidence gives you permission to say "NO" when you know it's not the right thing for you to do. Confidence is never belittling to others, in fact it is what gives you the ability to take others along with you and share the joy and happiness of success. Just because you choose to opt out due to your own convictions does not mean that you are a bad person, it does not mean you are selfish. It just means that you know yourself enough to choose to follow your own rules and your own path.

I wish I had a nickel for every time someone told me about a job or a position that they think I would be great at. You should be a salesperson again, you should be in banking, and you should be in politics. I've heard them all. I know that the only thing that I really want to do is coaching. I LOVE seeing people self-discover and make break-throughs that change their lives. It's the only profession I want at this point in my life. I have the skills, the education and the true commitment to the profession that will not only be financially rewarding to me, but will bring me peace, contentment and fulfillment. To take a job doing something otherwise wouldn't be fair to an employer. I would definitely not reach maximum results. My heart and my being would not be into it the way that it would need to be. I would be out of complete alignment with myself, my values, my purpose and I would definitely NOT be able to be in my power. That's how it works.

Everyone knows when they are not "living the life they can't wait to live". It feels all wrong. If you know yourself and seize your power, it's impossible to settle for anything less! And you don't have to.

As I work through this 50th year, I hope that I am able to share this one little concept with as many people as possible because I do believe that it is the one thing that makes all the difference. If I would have known then, what I know now, that is what I would share. You only have one life. Many people, employers, family members and friends will be there with you as you pave your path. Some will come and go, but you will have

...for the Future Woman

yourself for the entire journey. Stay true to what your heart and mind tell you is right. Educate yourself in anything you can that will build your skill, learn from mentors who have already gone before you and most of all, put it all into conscious action. You are either living in your power, working toward your goals, OR YOU ARE NOT. Always be honest with yourself and never make excuses to try to make YOU believe otherwise.

Make yourself your best companion, KNOW YOURSELF and SEIZE YOUR POWER...FIRST, be your own best advocate and the person who stands up for you in confidence in all of your choices and ventures. If you do this one little thing, "KNOW YOURSELF AND SEIZE YOUR POWER...FIRST", you will find that you have created your life by design, NOT by default or the will of others. You will be happy, you will be at peace and you will THRIVE!

My Now...

Becky L. Goodwin

Becky is a banking executive with 22+ years of experience within the regulatory and private financial industry. She most recently served as a SVP and part of the Strategic Leadership Team at a large banking organization Becky spent several years at the Federal Reserve Bank of Philadelphia. She also served in numerous leadership roles at both HSBC Bank USA and JPMorgan over the course of her professional career.

During her time at the Federal Reserve Bank of Philadelphia, she served as an instructor for both FFIEC classes and the Diversity and Inclusion mandated course. Becky also served on the supporting Committee of The Office of Minority and Women Inclusion while at the Federal Reserve.

Becky earned her Bachelor of Science in Management Science from Coppin State University in Baltimore, Maryland. In later years, she obtained her MBA in Executive Leadership from Wesley College in New Castle, Delaware.

Becky is student mentor, when time permits. She is also a published author of several regulatory articles in SRC Insights, a former FRB publication, and a contributing author in a book for students titled "My Now for the Student Leader." Becky enjoys writing and performing spoken word poetry and has an affinity for nature.

… for the Future Woman

The Inner Compass
Becky L. Goodwin

This chapter is designed to stop you in your tracks and ultimately give you pause to think about what you want to accomplish. I will share with you over the next few pages attributes of a well-tuned inner compass that will keep you grounded and prevent you from wasting years in a wishing well, wallowing in self-pity or from the weighty task of carrying grudges that prevent you from excelling on the path of success. I define the inner compass as the breeding ground for motivation, desires, and emotions. There are times in everyone's life when circumstances overwhelm us and our inner compass goes out of good working order. Those occurrences are normal and to be expected; however, when we allow ourselves to function for long periods of time in an imbalanced state, we can do irrevocable harm to ourselves and others unknowingly.

Quietly know thyself

Are you driving the vehicle called life or is life driving you? In other words, are you generally headed in a self-directed, goal oriented direction or are you just floating through life? Are you generally aware of your desires, short and long term or do your desires change with the direction of the wind? Thirdly, are you emotionally sound and secure with who you are or do allow yourself to be easily moved by the opinions and actions of others? If you identified more with the latter part in any of the preceding questions, you will want to fine tune your inner compass.

Tuning your inner compass begins with understanding your strength, desires and knowing what motivates you personally. There have been many who have said finding your purpose is the key to discovering what motivates you or vice versa. Oprah is quoted as saying "Understand that the right to choose your own path is a sacred privilege. Use it. Dwell in possibility."[1] Tuning your inner compass is essential to discovering a productive road and staying on track.

Quiet meditative time is a building block in that regard. Rarely do we get time in today's wired, noisy hectic society to just quiet down and think. Decluttering your mind routinely is as critical as clearing your living space. We are often hoarders in our own mind. Meditation, prayer, stretching, de-plugging and scheduling quiet time is essential to tuning the inner compass. Hal Elrod, the author of The Miracle Morning (Elrod, Hal, 2012) indicated that "your morning routine or lack thereof dramatically affects the levels of success in every area of your life." I am

---

[1] http://www.oprah.com/spirit/Thought-for-Today-Independence

finding out in my forties, that Hal is accurate in that assessment. My greatest successes and creativity are directly correlated with quiet meditative time spent and a disciplined routine. As you read this chapter think about harnessing the power of each morning. Use the time to get to know you, improve yourself and define your unique path to success.

Journal the vision/Visualize your achievements

Great ideas are fleeting, of this I am certain. How many times have you had a great idea and later discovered that you could not remember the idea. A cluttered mind is like a cluttered house or office, you will eventually misplace something important and it may cost you. There is power in journaling your dreams and plans. People now frequently journal and create vision boards. Journaling is simply a way of getting your thoughts and ideas on paper. It is also a good practice to include positive affirmations daily. Recite them in the mirror for instantaneous confidence. I will share some thoughts later about organizing those thoughts.

There is something about getting your thoughts on paper that allow for creativity to flow. My first experience with this concept came after I had lost my Aunt Maggie. It was very painful and I needed an outlet for the pain. I prayed earnestly about it and the next day when I awoke, I immediately grabbed a pen and began to write. The poetic piece that poured out of me was titled "Mountain Move." It was a gift given to me by the creator. I actually recited the poem at my Aunt's funeral and it was then that I discovered I had the gift for spoken word poetry. Spoken word poetry still serves as an outlet for my creativity.

Whether you take up journaling for poetry, thought generation or ideas it can certainly serve as a launching pad for greater possibilities. Some folk's journal their dreams by jotting them down immediately, because dreams, like thoughts can be fleeting. The power of a thought is powerful; after all, this keyboard that I am typing upon was once a thought. Imagine that.

Vision boards are another popular outlet for creativity and planning. Vision boards are used to generate feelings that are motivating and truly capture the essence of who you want to be and what you want to accomplish based on what you visualize. According to an article in the Huffington Post, vision boards actually work and have been used by Olympic athletes to improve performance.[2] Vision boards are based on the premise that one attracts what they think about or visualize. Vision boards filled with your goals visualized are designed to help you really focus on what you desire for your life. Subsequently your thoughts about those things you envision are attracted to you and vice versa. Pinterest® serves as a modern day digital Vision

---

[2] http://www.huffingtonpost.com/elizabeth-rider/the-scientific-reason-why_b_6392274.html

board for many people today. I encourage you to do the research and start small; you may surprise yourself in a good way.

Develop discipline

Both procrastination and lack of organization can be costly. Practice good habits, and wane yourself from unproductive or otherwise bad habits while you have youth on your side. This is probably the most challenging advice I can render. I have discovered that an abundance of talent, skill, or influence serves as a launching pad or door opener; but, discipline is needed for sustainability and longevity in any worthwhile pursuit. A staple in everyone's library who aims for sustainable success should be The Seven Habits of Highly Effective People by Stephen R. Covey. (Covey, Stephen R., 1989) This book will remind you of the importance of centering yourself for the purpose of successfully fulfilling your destiny. Pursue excellence in all you do, I can assure you someone will notice!

This too shall pass: Dealing with disappointment, doubt and fear

Allowing yourself to feel, but not allowing those feelings to dictate your reaction is a balancing act you will have to master with time and experience. Organizing your thoughts helps tremendously in this regard. You will assuredly have disappointments, setbacks and losses. Some folks never recover from criticism, rejection or lost opportunities. Be quick to forgive, it frees you from the quicksand of mediocrity and animosity, the twins of assured failure and lost opportunities. Emotionally intelligent people are thought to have mastered this concept exceptionally well. Emotional intelligence is also a sought after commodity in leadership roles. Align yourself with the people who will invest in your success, opportunities and upward mobility. Affirm out loudly and often, if you must (you should) your worthiness, ability and strength. I hope this chapter has encouraged you to discover your inner compass! Tune it both well and frequently. Remember both your thoughts and words have power. Finally understand that some feelings are temporal, give yourself time to feel, time to heal, and time to focus and reclaim your balance on this wonderful God given journey called life. Know thyself well!

...for the Future Woman

My Now...

Tanya A. Hollins

Tanya Hollins is a dynamic business professional with more than 20 years of diverse management experience. Ms. Hollins has held key leadership positions in the healthcare, financial services, and education management industries. Her business acumen, innovative spirit, and passion for education and training are the founding principles of her approach to leadership and the development thereof. Through the years, Tanya has successfully established, motivated, and managed centralized teams whose efforts resulted in streamlined operations and organizational efficiencies.

Ms. Hollins is committed to working with today's youth and mentoring tomorrow's business leaders. Tanya has a natural ability to build relationships and effortlessly connect with others. She attributes these abilities as her formula for success. Ms. Hollins is often quoted as saying "If it's effortless, it's right".

Tanya holds a Bachelor's degree in Accounting from the University of Alabama-Huntsville and a Master's in Business Administration from Samford University.

Contact Tanya at thollinsmba@gmail.com

...for the Future Woman

A Woman's Work is Her Worth
Tanya A. Hollins

How many times have you heard the phrase "a woman's work is never done"? When you hear someone say it, how does it speak to your heart? I often remember hearing that phrase as a young girl and instantly thinking that womanhood and the responsibility that would accompany it would be daunting. But, as I became much older and much wiser, I developed a very different and more positive interpretation of that phrase. The new and deeper meaning for me was that a woman's role in society was amazingly powerful and continuously evolving. I began to get excited and celebrate womanhood. I quickly learned that each one of us has a unique purpose in life to fulfill. What an awesome gift from above! And once you truly understand your purpose, you can begin your life's work. Your work as a woman will include developing a strong faith and belief system, maintaining and creating healthy relationships, obtaining a good education, maintaining optimal health, and taking an interest in your local community and the community at large. All of these elements are key life principles when put into practice are instrumental in building self-confidence, developing self-worth and becoming a dynamic woman who can effect change and make a difference in the world. Simply stated, your work defines your worth.

Have Faith. Wikipedia defines faith as "confidence or trust in a person or thing or a belief not based on proof". Faith is a principle of action and power. Whenever you work toward a particular goal in life, you are exercising faith. In pursuit of the goal, you demonstrate hope for something that you haven't seen or experienced yet. Faith is so powerful that it can serve many purposes in your life. As women, we are naturally strong and resilient human beings. Often times, we may not realize exactly how strong we are until we experience a difficult life event. I honestly believe the inner strength we possess is a direct correlation to the depth of our faith. The level of faith in God or a higher power that you have will establish your foundation in life. And it's so important to build your foundation on solid, stable ground. Once the foundation has been established, your faith and belief system will provide you with direction and guide you along life's journey. Think of faith as a point on your moral compass. Your faith serves as the inner voice that helps you discern right from wrong. Faith will allow you to appreciate and be grateful for the good times and successes in life. And faith will sustain you when you encounter difficulties or challenges in life. The sustaining power of faith will erase all doubt, eliminate fear and enable you to have a positive outlook despite the current circumstances. A positive outlook on life helps you make good choices for the amazing woman you were created to become.

Maintaining and Creating Healthy Relationships. Healthy relationships can be fulfilling, worthwhile and inspirational. You absolutely can have healthy relationships with anyone in your life--family members, friends, classmates, co-workers, and love interests. You must put in the work upfront because relationship building requires much effort and continuous nurturing. As women, we are naturally loving and nurturing. It's in our DNA. With that said, it's important to maintain a healthy balance in all of your relationships—existing and new. Equal amounts of give and take must occur for all parties involved. This shared responsibility is accompanied by the following must haves: trust, mutual respect, and the ability to openly communicate with one another. Each individual in the relationship must demonstrate trust and respect in order for the relationships to thrive. Although you may experience disagreements, all parties involved in the relationship should always be able to openly express feelings and resolve differences without a rush to judgement. As a woman, it's particularly important to develop and maintain healthy relationships with others. Your inner circle will be your most important support system. Your circle will celebrate your successes and encourage you through challenging times. You should always feel good about yourself when you are interacting with those you are in relationship with. And you should feel safe to entrust them on some level with your secrets, your life goals and your dreams. If at any point in a relationship you experience significant feelings of fear, disrespect, or distrust, it's absolutely critical that you assert yourself. Be clear and direct in expressing your thoughts and feelings about the situation. Try your best to resolve the issues in a manner that is mutually respectful of all parties involved. If you are unable to resolve differences and continue the connection in a healthy way, then it is time to seriously re-evaluate the relationship. Always know and understand that it's okay if you need to alter the dynamic of the relationship or even resort to closing the door completely on the relationship. Remember, good self-care and strong self-love are requirements for the health and success of any relationship.

Invest in Your Education. Higher education is one of the most worthwhile pursuits in life. An education will open many doors of opportunity for you. Renowned polymath Benjamin Franklin once said "An investment in knowledge pays the best interest". Knowledge truly is power and earning your education is an investment in your future. As with any investment, there's always an upfront cost. That cost includes financial resources and personal commitment. Take time to plan ahead and plan wisely. Seek guidance from a mentor. Identify your educational goals and what you desire to accomplish. Carefully research various academic programs. Explore ground and online campus options to determine which forum of learning will work best for you. Analyze your current resources, and investigate scholarships and other opportunities for financial assistance. Once you have all of the data required to make a good decision regarding how and where you will pursue your education, take the next step and enroll in school. The U.S. economy has experienced a tremendous shift and it is now one that is primarily based upon knowledge. A woman's role in society has also changed significantly and it continues to evolve exponentially. Today's educated woman is highly respected and recognized as a key contributor and leader in the workplace. Keep in mind there are both tangible and intangible rewards to getting your education. With a good education, you can become a successful entrepreneur or secure a well-paying job and ultimately launch an exciting career. The knowledge you gain today will promote your continued intellectual development, foster your exploration of new ideas, and enable you to effect significant change in the world.

Commit to Health & Wellness. A healthy body and a healthy mind are two of the greatest assets a woman can have. As women, we play a pivotal role in our homes, in the community and in the workplace. There are many who depend upon us for wisdom, guidance, leadership, and encouragement. To that end, we have a responsibility to maintain good health so that we can continue to be available for those who may need us. Making a personal commitment to living a healthy lifestyle requires motivation and discipline. Discipline plus consistency equals results. I strongly encourage you to create an exercise routine that will work for your daily life. Adopt a healthy diet and make good food choices each day. Heathy eating and regular exercise go hand in hand. The healthy lifestyle you develop today will become second nature to you tomorrow. Through diet and exercise, you will be able to reduce health risks and perhaps prevent health challenges that primarily affect women such as heart disease, chronic fatigue and depression. Diet and exercise are good for your body and good for your mind. Medical research has proven that as you exercise, certain chemicals are released in your brain that make you feel good. The positive energy generated from regular exercise will boost self-esteem, improve feelings of self-worth, enhance concentration, and regulate sleep patterns. Physical activity also provides you with a well-deserved and much needed break from the fast paced and responsibility filled lives we often lead as women. Over time, you will look and feel fantastic which will enable you to inspire others to live healthy.

Lend a Helping Hand. American activist Marian Wright Edelman most eloquently said "Service is the rent we pay for living". And wouldn't the world be a much better, brighter place if everyone adopted and acted upon the principle of giving back and paying it forward? So, let it begin with you. Accept and embrace the responsibility of being concerned about the wellbeing of others. Develop a compassionate spirit of giving. Commit to enriching the lives of others. The act of giving will bring great joy and a better quality of life to someone in need.

...for the Future Woman

And giving can also prove to be emotionally and spiritually rewarding for you. Take time to research and connect with a charitable organization or support a worthy cause that you believe in. Consistently donate whatever and whenever you can. This includes donating a portion of your time, talents or resources. Even small acts of kindness can make big differences in the world as we know it. The power to make a difference belongs to you.

Embrace and Celebrate the Journey. You are the author of your journey to womanhood. You are the star of what will be an exciting story--your life story. Continue to develop and strengthen your faith. Take inventory of current relationships and strive to cultivate new connections that are healthy. Increase your knowledge and share what you learn with others. Maintain optimal physical and mental health through exercise and diet. Adopt a healthy lifestyle. Good life balance is so important. Develop a compassionate spirit and a willingness to help others. Discipline and personal commitment are required to create and maintain each one of these principles in your life. Yes, womanhood definitely comes with significant responsibility. But, to whom much is given, much shall be required. Celebrate you and the woman you are becoming. Stay focused and stay the course because anything worth having in life is certainly worth working for. The active presence and working of each principle in your life will continuously enhance your self-confidence and shape your character while also promoting

My Now…

beauty and harmony within your heart and soul. The key is to first know your purpose. After which, identify with each element of your life's work and allow the uniqueness of each element to become your life's worth. Get excited and embrace the journey. It's yours to behold!

...for the Future Woman

Sharon A. Myers

Sharon A. Myers is the Founder and CEO of Moovin4ward Presentations, an empowerment company that facilitates leadership development, and entrepreneurial programs for youth, students and professionals. She is the developer of several youth programs to include Journey to Success: Personal Success Strategic Plan (PSSP) Program, which is based on the book Mapping Your Journey to Success: Six Steps for Personal Planning. She has also developed the My Now Career & Leadership Conference and the Young Entrepreneur Success (YES!) Program.

sharon@moovin4ward.com
www.Moovin4ward.com
www.Moovin4wardTraining.com
www.Journey2SuccessPSSP.com
www.MyNowBooks.com
Tweet @moovin4ward

...for the Future Woman

Seeing is Believing
Sharon A. Myers

Growing up, I used to hear the term, "people say" as a justification for anything as truth. It is equivalent to folks today saying, "I read it on the Internet." But I eventually learned that whenever a statement is started with "people say..." or "I read on the Internet...", the rest is probably unfounded, unreliable, untrue, bullshit.

People said that I shouldn't be where I am today. But I'm here. Here's my story.

My early years started in the projects. My mother got pregnant as a freshman in college, married my young father, her high school sweetheart, and tried to make it work. After a couple of years, my mother was again living with my grandmother, my aunt, my young uncle and me. My grandmother, also divorced with kids, worked as a maid for several middle- and high-class households. And on the side, she sold liquor out of her home. It was a bootleg house... in the projects. Her customers drank their shots in her living-room. Needless to say, the house was frequently filled with loud-talking drunks and it was probably not the best environment for a preschooler. *People say* that children who are raised in this environment are destined to be stuck in this environment… doomed from moving forward.

Not true.

My grandmother was a God-fearing woman. Every Sunday, I got my hair greased and pressed, and put on a lacy dress with shiny black patent leather shoes for church. I sat with a big smile on my face next to my grandmother who always wore a big, pretty hat. My grandmother was doing what she needed to do to survive. She later saved enough to buy a three-bedroom house, with a yard, far away from public housing. She had a different future in mind, regardless of what *people said*.

We moved around quite a bit before I was 7 years old, and now I had a baby brother. My mom was young, single and trying desperately to keep us out of the projects and off welfare. This feat required her to work two jobs while trying to continue her college classes. She had been trying to finish college, one or two classes a year, since before I was born. *People say*, if you start college and drop out for any reason, you won't ever finish because you will likely no longer have the time or resources. But nearly 20 years later, she earned her degree.

My freshman year of high school, I had to choose between a *career-path* or *college-path* curriculum. Since my mama struggled to keep the refrigerator filled and I wasn't a studious kid, I chose

...for the Future Woman

the career path. *People say* that at-risk kids, who get free lunches and whose parents are on food-stamps, don't go to college. I knew my future would be bright, so I figured I would work my way up to it. I never even discussed the curriculum path with my mother.

A few months before graduation, my mom asked where I wanted to go to college. I was shocked, stunned, and confused. How am I going to go to college? She shared that I qualify for a Pell grant! Being a low income family meant I could go to college for almost free! I was excited and almost angry that I didn't know it sooner. I started planning my exit from Alabama to move to Texas for college. I was already working as a high school co-op student at NASA. Maybe I could transfer to the NASA installation in Houston. Unfortunately, since I had not taken the college path courses, I didn't have the best transcript for college admission and I struggled with my standardized test. I was not prepared. My options were now limited. But I was locally and conditionally accepted to Alabama A&M University. I majored in Computer Science. *People said* someone like me wouldn't go to or get into college. But I did.

Like my mother, I got pregnant and married to my high school sweetheart. He was two years older than me and didn't like the idea of me going off to college. He was afraid. His fear intentionally got me pregnant. His goal was that I would not leave him behind by becoming a college student and an eventual

My Now...

college grad. He wasn't planning to go to college. It wasn't because he had a single mom who was broke. He lived with both of his parents in a four-bedroom house with a den. He had two siblings who were college graduates before him. He just didn't have a desire to go to college. And now I'm pregnant. *People said* that by keeping the baby I had just kissed my future goodbye. One lady told me that I'd never get my education; never get a good job; and would live on welfare and food stamps. I would struggle to raise my son alone.

I thought about that. Then I thought about the other things *people said* wouldn't happen... that did. My grandmother went from the projects to a three-bedroom house by cleaning houses and selling shots. My mother graduated from college after dropping out, as a single mother of two, while working two jobs. And now, I am in college. I've already started to envision how my future would be even brighter than the generations before me. So I don't care what that woman says. I don't care what *people say*. *I say* I'm going to keep moving forward anyway.

I didn't stay married for long. But I worked full time, went to school at night, and relied heavily on my family to help with my son. My ex was no help. He'd rather be jobless than to help me. So, I lived in some harsh neighborhoods in my effort to live independently, but I was willing to make the sacrifice. I was convinced that I still had a chance to have the future I believed was for me and my son. I was determined that I would not become a statistic of the repressive system. No one was going to tell me where I'd end up. No one was going to tell me what was in store for my future.

Twenty-five years later, I also have a Masters degree, and so does my mother. I'm working for a fortune 500 company and managing two small businesses that I started. My husband and I own a beautiful home and have a beautiful family with four kids and two grandkids. I had a *vision* of where I wanted to be in life, and a true *belief* that I would get here. I stopped listening to what *people said*.

Vision & Belief

Imagine a people who live in a cave. From one generation to the next, this community "under the rocks" is home for hundreds of people who have never seen the light of day. They were happy and content with their stony home. One day, a young girl questioned the origin of the water that seeps through the cracks each day to fill their small water holes. There was always enough for the community to drink and bathe, until the day that it flooded. It wasn't the first time that it flooded, but it was the first time in her lifetime. This made her very curious. She began to envision that there was lots and lots of water... somewhere. She started dreaming of plunging into a wide, vast, and unlimited body of water. But the *people said*, "no."

My Now...

This situation calls for a leader. A leader has the ability to communicate his/her vision and inspire others to believe in it. Seeing is believing, even when not tangible. So she shared her vision with a couple of friends. But this time she was able to paint a picture of the body of water in their minds and what it would feel like. They began to believe. She continued sharing and more people believed. Soon, she had the whole cave talking about this massive body of water that NO ONE had ever seen. So a plan was developed to dig their way TO it, just next to the small crack in the wall. They worked tirelessly for weeks, months, even years, digging. Some stopped believing. Even the girl, now a teen, started to doubt herself. Too much time, too many dead ends. "She's too young to understand the truth", the *people said*. But she continued to have the dreams each night of the water, which kept her vision constantly on her mind. With that, she was able to keep a small group of people motivated to keep moving forward by constantly refreshing the vision in their minds.

Eventually, the wall caved in. A gush of water flooded the cave. The people took to higher ground within the cave for days. Once the waters calmed and slowly lowered, everyone was amazed to see the enormous puddle that filled their home. They waded through the water to reach beyond the walls. They were amazed that there *was* an "other" side... a bigger other side. They looked up to see an infinitely large, dark blue sky, which was filled with blinking lights surrounding a bright and glowing ball. It was beautiful. Below, reflecting the sky lights, was an ocean of water. While it was far more than the girl ever dreamed, the vision that she believed in was truth.

This was not a real story, that I know of. But there are countless others:

1. Harriet Tubman believed that slaves should and could be free.
2. Martin Luther King believed that African Americans and European Americans could live together in harmony without prejudice.
3. Barack Obama believed that an African-American boy from a single white mother could be president.

In every case, there were some who didn't see it. And because they couldn't see it, they didn't believe it could happen. And because they didn't believe it could happen, they tried to talk the dreamer out of it. Sharon Myers believed that she could obtain higher education, raise a family with a spouse, own businesses and become a corporate executive... even if she was a black girl from the projects.

Don't allow others, who don't or can't see your vision or dreams, to convince you that they are not real or realizable. When you hit dead ends, kick it up a notch. This is when you have to press harder... regardless of what you read on the Internet or what *people say*.

My Now...

...for the *Future Woman*

Part 2: My Plan

My Now...

Vandria Steward

Growing up in the small town of Ruffin, South Carolina, I gained my foundation along with valuable life experiences, that led to the discovery of my purpose, which is to be an example of God's love. I give much appreciation to my beautiful parents, Benjamin and Owillinda Steward, for planting seeds that contributed towards my passion for helping others and being a positive voice, which works hand-in-hand with my purpose. These passions have afforded me many opportunities to meet people from various walks of life and at different stages and ages of life too. My volunteer experiences, ordered by GOD, have given me growth mentally and spiritually. Among these experiences, I not only have been blessed to mentor young people, but I've also spent countless hours serving at soup kitchens and after school programs along with offering a friendly source of comfort to hospice patients in my community.

...for the Future Woman

Accepting the STAR Power Within

Vandria Steward

We live in a world that exists to define and predict who we should be and how we should be in order to be accepted by the majority. There are trends that are adopted by the "popular" crowd to help categorize and decipher what is cool or not and what is "in or out". Does the world really have the final say or RIGHT to define who you are?

I grew up pondering these questions too. I know what it's like to feel the weight of imposed judgment and opinion. The voice that never had a mute button. The voice that doesn't have a filter, offer tact, respect, or consideration. I'm sure many of you have heard that uninvited voice. It offers unexpected feedback, it can possibly hurt feelings, and can even make you doubt your thoughts of yourself. It can directly challenge your self-esteem especially if it gives off negative energy. It's the kind of energy that makes you feel small and unimportant. It can also appear to be so strong, powerful and influential that it can make you question your existence because of the lack of acceptance that you've encountered, but is acceptance important? Everyone in some fashion wants to be recognized, seen, heard and acknowledged by another, but what's the price or sacrifice to have it? Is it worth following trends and changing who you are designed and created to be to gain that acceptance?

I had to answer similar questions for myself. It all started with me addressing that voice directly and head on. Was that voice that I couldn't escape beneficial or harmful to me? Was that voice important enough for me to feed into and adhere to? My answer was no. I learned that the negative voice(s) of the world, society, peers, family, friends, strangers and the like, ONLY had importance if I allowed it to. I consciously chose to NOT to give it power. I had to virtually realize I had NO CONTROL over those voices, but I had control of my thoughts and what I internalized. This is the day I discovered my voice and began to love and accept myself. This is the moment I gave my voice priority over the noise in the background.

How do you reflect with your inner voice? The person who looks in the mirror daily to pick himself or herself apart according to the judgment of what others think or say. The person who walks with his or her head down because they feel they are unworthy of a compliment or acknowledgement. The person who hides from the world because he or she is afraid or insecure that he or she doesn't look, sound or act the part to fit in. You whomever feels you aren't smart enough, small enough, pretty enough, lovable enough, talented enough, strong and powerful enough or whatever you think you lack. I need you to put an end

...for the Future Woman

to whatever makes you feel less of anything to realize YOU ARE ENOUGH! You are created and designed perfectly to be you. You ARE smart, beautiful, talented, lovable, strong and powerful enough. You are ALREADY equipped to be everything you desire to be. No one has the right to define, redefine or diminish what makes you GREAT! You are AMAZING, AWESOME, and FABULOUS in your own right. You are magnificently created by GOD. You are an original masterpiece that is uniquely created to SHINE like the STAR you already are! You are born with star power! You own star power! You exude star power whether you're aware of it or not! Your light maybe a little dim, but you have to find your switch to brighten your shine. You have been given your own special gifts to bring to the world that only you can deliver. You don't have to compete to be judged and wait to see if you have what it takes. You don't have to emulate, copy or try to be anyone else because you ALREADY have "it". You are naturally born with "it". You have to know and believe it's within you. You can allow it to shine to influence, encourage and help others. You are on this earth with a purpose to not only just exist but to be a blessing to the world.

You are not only uniquely special with a gift, but it's also important to know that each of you has a voice. Your voice is a gift that deserves to be heard. Your voice is a powerful tool that can speak volumes, help encourage change, make a difference and/ or bring awareness. No one has the right to silence your voice but you. Know that you have the power within to take a stand if necessary and bring notice to things that are important. You have been created to be put in the right place, at the right time, in the midst of the right situations and circumstances for only you to take notice and be a voice. Your voice is created to fit in but you must make the choice to be heard.

Now that you know what it takes to achieve star power you still have miles to conquer before your journey ends. The second half is putting these gifts and voices to good use. You do this by finding your platform, putting your creativity to the test, finding what interest you the most, exercising your talents and or doing whatever it takes to make use of what you've been gifted with to be purposeful to the world. If you're unsure of what you have to offer, take the time to discover your gifts. What areas do you shine in the most? What do you enjoy doing? Make a list to help you narrow things down. You may be good at singing, caring for others, giving advice, organizing, business, planning events and sports just to name a few things. Everyone has been given a gift in life, you have to find where you shine. If you need help, seek assistance from someone such as a guidance counselor, someone in the area of career services or possibly a life coach. A family member or friend can also be of assistance to help you acknowledge what you may be overlooking when it comes to your gifts and talents. If you already know what you're good at, the next step would be to learn as much as possible about the area, to advance and find ways to grow. There are millions of resources that can provide you with information. Your public library offers numerous free sources to assist you in your research. You may pursue this area in higher education as an option to gain more insight and hands on experience. You can also find a mentor in the area of interest, to learn from others who have traveled the path you desire to travel. A mentor can offer advice, tips and testimonial stories to help you decide if you're making the right choice and provide first hand insight. You can volunteer your time in your area of interest, to not only gain experience, skills and credibility but also give back to the community. The greatest gift in mastering and becoming great at something is that you return the gift in the future to someone else who is trying to find their purpose and voice. This is the recycle of leadership, love and sisterhood/brotherhood. Everything you learn and gain should be with the purpose to someday pass it along to keep the cycle going.

All that has been shared narrows down to a personal choice. That personal choice starts with you making the decision to be comfortable being you. You must make the choice to accept your individuality and your voice. You must personally embrace what has been authentically designed for you only. You must find a way to accept you before anyone else does. You don't need the cosign of anyone else to validate how important, relevant and valuable you are. When you know your value, you set the bar for how others treat, respect and view you. When you know, believe and have the confidence to share with the world what you

My Now...

have to offer, you contribute towards making the world a better place. You have a purpose and destiny designated to the name that has been granted to you. Only you can fulfill it and carry it out. No one else can carry out the plan or purpose meant for you. The world needs you. The world awaits you, but the world doesn't define you. The world will always exist before and after you, but will you make the choice to offer and gift it with what only you can provide. You are ENOUGH! You already have "it". Be the star you are and take your place where you deserve shine.

...for the Future Woman

My Now...

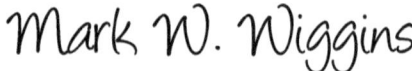
Mark W. Wiggins

Mark "The Speaker Man" Wiggins, an International speaker, trainer, author and entrepreneur is the CEO of Xtreme Effort Speaking. He has held leadership and management positions within several national retail companies, such as Foot Locker, Eddie Bauer, and Levi Strauss & Co. He has trained corporate, community, and association leaders in the Washington, DC area on the topics of customers, leadership and human performance.

He is the author of *Permission to Succeed: the Only Person Who Needs to Give it is You*; *MTXE the Formula for Success*; and more. He is also one of the featured authors of the book, *My Vision, My Plan, My NOW!*

Get my information right now! Text the word "Speakerman" to 90210
Email: Mark@markthespeakerman.com
Tweet: @Speakerman87

...for the Future Woman

Kryptonite

Mark Wiggins

Without question or hesitation, when you mention the word Kryptonite, you think of Superman. The Man of Steel, able to leap buildings with a single bound, faster than a speeding bullet.... And you know the rest. But for all his strength and the seemingly indestructible power, he has one weakness – yes, Kryptonite. There are many theories as to what Kryptonite actually does to weaken Superman, but I will offer one that makes sense. Superman's power comes from the earth's sun, much like a solar cell. If the solar cell is blocked, then there is less power. Kryptonite does this in a basic sense. It blocks the sun's rays and keeps him from being charged up to his fullest potential. Surprisingly, this act of blocking leads to him being rendered mortal and average. But when he knows there is a possibility for it to be present, he plans accordingly and avoids it all together. Either that or Lois Lane shows up to unwittingly save the day.

The concept of being weakened by someone or something has worked its way into the lexicon. Urban Dictionary has listed this as one of its many definitions of Kryptonite:

My Now…

A man/woman that calls someone their Kryptonite means that they are their weakness. Someone or something they have to stay away from because they want it even though it's not good for them or will hurt them.

There are other great heroes and mythical characters that have weaknesses. Achilles, for example, had his whole body dipped into river Styx – all except his heel, thus creating the term "Achilles' heel". A small yet vulnerable spot that, if exploited, can bring this mighty mythical character to his knees. Sampson is another great Biblical Character that was actually misrepresented in his super strength, if you will. People get it twisted and think that his hair was his Kryptonite, and that, if you cut it, he would lose his power. That is not Kryptonite, by definition because Kryptonite is defined as someone or something that causes one to lose their power. Sampson's Kryptonite was his ego, strength, and lust for women that ultimately cost him his power, temporarily. Delilah may have caused him to be tricked into getting his hair cut – his outward sign of strength – but if you read further in the story, Sampson's hair grew back, as it should. Like with most super heroes, they may be weakened but somehow they manage to get their strength back and continue the fight.

Lastly for the ladies.

...for the *Future Woman*

Diana Prince, also known as the Amazon princess, Wonder Woman. Wonder Woman has three different types of Kryptonite, if you will: piercing objects, like a spear or an arrow, if her bangles, which are used to deflect those piercing objects, are tied together she is rendered helpless, and lastly she can be the victim of her own Lasso of truth. So for her, something that is considered her strength when not used correctly can actually be her kryptonite. Well, at least Wonder Woman had the cool invisible jet.

So what is your Kryptonite? What is it that can block you from your power source, or side-track you from your dream? Could it be your friends or a group of people that, when you get with them, they seem to suck all of your time up and cause you delays in what you do? Is it the fear of success, self-doubt, candy, overeating or too much exercise? Whatever it is, you need to be able to identify it so you can manage it, and not have it manage you.

I have a friend who models and does trade shows, print ads, etc. She is an older model, and dare I say non-traditional in the modeling sense. She, by all accounts, has a very good career. However, she spends about 3-4 hours a day in the gym. If she misses a day she begins to rant and rave about how she is going to lose her figure. Her Kryptonite, isn't not working out, her kryptonite is actually anything that keeps her from working out. Whether it is a trip, or family stuff, she begins to feel like she is losing the edge, after one whole day. She then tries to overcompensate for that day on the next visit to the gym.

Kryptonite can be seen as anything that keeps you weak or distracted from your purpose. What things in your life would you label as kryptonite? Now some of these things are not bad but when introduced at the wrong time they can hinder your progress. Just like with Wonder woman. Her Lasso of Truth works great, but when turned on her, it renders her helpless and she cannot lie, potentially revealing secrets to the whereabouts of the invisible jet.

So how do you deal with kryptonite? How can you protect yourself from its harmful effect? Who will know your secret and try to use it against you? Well first of all, you must acknowledge that you have kryptonite-y type issues that hinder your growth. Take an inventory of things that you are doing, and when you should or shouldn't be doing that thing to help you get to the next level. Sometimes TV is my Kryptonite. For me, it's ESPN, the world-wide leader in sports, specifically. I am a sucker for Sports Center, each and every time it comes on, all morning. I will watch it like I didn't see the reply the first three times. I used to have cable, with 299 channels, and I would only watch the ESPN family of channels – yes even the Spanish version for fun. What a waste of time. I noticed that when I wanted to work at home I had to have on some background noise, something that didn't require me to pay full attention to but still allows me to focus on my work. Well, when its basketball season that is hard to do, but I tried. I knew when I flipped it on, it was over. Kryptonite. So what did I do? I got rid of cable, went to streaming TV, and now I can catch all of my favorite shows when I want – I am no longer a slave to the time slot. Superman had to tell someone that he and kryptonite don't get along, so when they were around or it showed up, in the nick of time they knew what to do to help Superman regain his power. Take a lesson from him and get a support system. The only way you beat kryptonite is to get away from it as fast as you can, even if it means turning off your cell phone. What?!?

Here are some types of Kryptonite and how they weaken your performance. I spoke with some very successful people and asked them what their kryptonite is and how they handle it. Check this out and see if any sound like you and see what you can do to fix it.

Fear of success, fear of failure, family, anger, selfishness, over planning, frustration, lack of support, broadcasting, procrastination, social media, adult ADD. The list goes on.

Those are just some of the many forms of Kryptonite. The fact of the matter is that you have to find yours and figure out the best way to manage or overcome yours. Here are some tips to guide you:

1. Acknowledge that certain things take you off track

2. Learn the signs and when they show up
3. Get a mentor or a life or business coach
4. Work to get over the issues by being real with yourself
5. Set smaller mid-range goals
6. Learn to refocus
7. Learn to delegate
8. Visualization
9. Family
10. Friends

Another thing you can do is get a mentor or find a support group. The saying, "birds of a feather flock together" is very true. Here is why its works. When birds of the same species fly together they get further with less effort. I was watching a Discovery Channel documentary of migrating birds. They can fly around the world to get back to the mating place, and they are able to fly for days over water with no land in sight by being in formation, drafting and taking turns leading the flock. If you are not around likeminded people, you will be dragging and pulling everything yourself and it tires you out and you want to quit. Find networking groups of people who are looking to be successful and understand the issues you may have. When I had my cookie business, it was hard to sit around with my friends and discuss my business concerns like payroll, drivers, the employees, etc. You cannot talk about work force with your friends who maybe make up someone's work force. Not cool. But if you were with

...for the Future Woman

some other folks that were likeminded, then it would be an easier conversation and you may find some solutions as well.

Allow time for some kryptonite in your life without guilt. It would be foolish to say you should completely avoid your kryptonite as if it is a bad thing. Kryptonite can sneak up on you, and thwart the best of your plans.

As I bring this to a close, I just want to say that hopefully you don't get the wrong idea about Kryptonite. In my application, it's not life threating – it can even be fun. However, if it takes away from your dreams and your success, then it needs to be monitored. Sometimes Kryptonite can hurt, and it can be memories of past failures or hurts or disappointment or friends that let you down. If you read Permission to Succeed: The only person who needs to give it is you, I talked about the Whispers. That's the little voice inside you that tries to convince you that you cannot do it. It proceeds to bring to mind all of the reasons that you should not try it again, or finish, or even attempt whatever you dream is. Success hinges on YOUR effort. Not what others say or how they co-sign. Please take Kryptonite seriously. Superman had to, so you should as well.

Thanks for reading. Here is my FREE GIFT to you. Text the word "Speakerman" to 90210 to get your FREE audio copy of Permission to Succeed: The only person who needs to give it is YOU!

#GETOFFTHEBENCH

Andrea Foy

Andrea Foy is an award-winning international author, speaker, consultant and coach. She conducts workshops and seminars on topics such as: Women's Issues, Business Skills, Diversity, Image Consulting, Personal Success Strategic Plan and the Hire Power Series. Andrea is a Certified Professional Coach, a Certified Diversity Training Consultant and a Certified Facilitator with Moovin4ward Presentations. She is also an Independent John Maxwell Leadership Coach.

You can reach Andrea at info@andreafoy.com or visit her website at www.andreafoy.com.

...for the Future Woman

Protecting the Future You... Now

Andrea Foy

My message to the future woman is that I want her to be able to understand how to protect herself; body, mind and soul. As we strive to grow into womanhood and become independent, we may forget or think we don't need all the advice we've learned on how to protect ourself. Some of us don't know or have forgot the little things. Here is some advice on dating, dining, and domestic violence. Even if you don't go to college, it is similar to living by yourself for the first time. Here is a reminder/primer of the little things.

The National Crime Prevention Council has an informative website dealing with women's safety. Here is my synopsis of the some of the information.

Dating

- ☑ When meeting for the first time, never allow your date to pick you up from your home.
- ☑ Consider going out with a group of people, or a double date. Come with the girls; leave with the girls.

- ☑ **Pay your way on the first date.** Or go Dutch.
- ☑ Never go to someone's room, apartment or house that you just met.
- ☑ Provide your own transportation to your public meeting place and make sure you have more than enough gas.
- ☑ Avoid going to secluded areas such as parks.
- ☑ Be careful how much you drink, if anything, in restaurants or bars as well. If you are alone; men may be watching you imbibe.
- ☑ Don't accept beverages from someone you don't know, it is often interpreted as an invitation.
- ☑ **Trust your instincts, if it doesn't feel right, it probably isn't.**
- ☑ Never give personal information to people that you don't know (name, home address, phone number, etc.).
- ☑ Use a nickname in chat rooms or message boards.
- ☑ **Use a separate free Email account.**
- ☑ **Consider using a different Cell Phone -** if you can afford it, get a Cricket pre-paid card for the same reasons above.
- ☑ **Beware of married men!**

This is usually a man who, when you ask "Are you married?" he repeats the word as if he never heard of it. I know a woman who made a man show her his divorce papers before she went out with him. I went on a date with a man who was separated from his wife. Only she still lived in his house and was pregnant at the time! I also went to dinner with a man who was 'separated.' His wife had taken his daughter to Europe for her graduation present! Sigh!

Drugs

- ☑ Rohypnol and GHB are called "date rape drugs" because when they are slipped into someone's drink, a sexual assault can occur without the victim being able to remember what happened.
- ☑ Rohypnol *(roofies, roopies, circles, the forget pills)* works like a tranquilizer. It causes muscle weakness, fatigue, slurred speech, loss of motor coordination and judgment, and amnesia that lasts up to 94 hours. It looks like aspirin—small, white, and round.
- ☑ GHB *(liquid X, salt water, scoop)* causes quick sedation. Its effects are drowsiness, nausea, vomiting, headaches, dizziness, coma, and death. The most common form is a clear liquid, although it also can be a white, grainy powder.
- ☑ Communication - Make sure the men in your life understand about what, if any, sexual behavior you are comfortable with and keep talking as you get deeper into a relationship.

- ☑ If you think you've been sexually assaulted under the influence of a date rape drug, get medical help immediately. Try not to urinate before providing any urine samples. If possible, collect any containers from which you drank.
- ☑ Trust your gut feelings. If a place or the way your date acts makes you nervous or uneasy, leave. Always have a cell phone and make sure it is fully charged. Have money for a cab.

Domestic Violence

What if he:

- ☑ Puts you down in front of friends or tells you that you would be nothing without him?
- ☑ Scares you? Makes you worry about reactions to things you say or do? Threatens you? Uses or owns weapons?
- ☑ Is violent? Has a history of fighting, loses his or her temper quickly, brags about mistreating others? Grabs, pushes, shoves, or hits you?
- ☑ Pressures you for sex or is forceful or scary about sex? Gets too serious about the relationship too fast?
- ☑ Abuses alcohol or other drugs and pressures you to use them?
- ☑ Has a history of failed relationships and always blames the other person for all of the problems?

- ☑ Believes that he should be in control of the relationship?
- ☑ Makes your family and friends uneasy and concerned for your safety?

You Want Out?

- ☑ Don't put up with abuse. You deserve better.
- ☑ Know that you are not alone. Teens from all different backgrounds across the country are involved in or have been involved in a violent relationship.
- ☑ Understand that you have done nothing wrong. It is not your fault.
- ☑ Know that the longer you stay in the abusive relationship, the more intense the violence will become.
- ☑ Recognize that being drunk is not an excuse for someone to become abusive.
- ☑ Talk with your parents, a friend, a counselor, a faith leader or spiritual leader, or someone else you trust. The more isolated you are from friends and family, the more control the abuser has over you.
- ☑ Know that you can get help from professionals at rape crisis centers, health services, counseling centers, or your family's health care provider.
- ☑ Alert a school counselor or security officer about the abuse.
- ☑ Keep a daily log of the abuse for evidence.

- ☑ Remember that no one is justified in attacking you just because he or she is angry.
- ☑ Do not meet him or her alone. Do not let him or her in your home or car when you are alone.
- ☑ Avoid being alone at school, your job, or on the way to and from places.
- ☑ Always tell someone where you are going and when you plan to be back.
- ☑ Plan and rehearse what you will do if he or she becomes abusive.

NATIONAL CRIME PREVENTION COUNCIL

www.ncpc.org

...for the Future Woman

Dater's Bill of Rights

- ☑ I have the right to refuse a date without feeling guilty.
- ☑ I can ask for a date without feeling rejected or inadequate if the answer is no.
- ☑ I do not have to act macho.
- ☑ I may choose not to act seductively.
- ☑ If I don't want physical closeness, I have the right to say so.
- ☑ I have the right to start a relationship slowly, to say,
- ☑ "I want to know you better before I become involved."
- ☑ I have the right to be myself without changing to suit others.
- ☑ I have the right to change a relationship when my feelings change. I can say, "We used to be close, but I want something else now."
- ☑ If I am told a relationship is changing, I have the right not to blame or change myself to keep it going.
- ☑ I have the right to an equal relationship with my partner.
- ☑ I have the right not to dominate or to be dominated.
- ☑ I have the right to act one way with one person and a different way with someone else.
- ☑ I have the right to change my goals whenever I want to.

NATIONAL CRIME PREVENTION COUNCIL

www.ncpc.org

My Now...

Nikia Brown-Sweeney

Nikia, Executive Director of Amani Nicol Incorporated (ANinc), has been an advocate for youth for over a decade. "Changing mindsets to change lives" is the vision that has inspired Nikia to motivate youth and women. Providing a platform for girls to believe that it's their unique traits and personality that makes them beautiful is the nucleus of the ANinc program for youths. Nikia's recent addition to the program features outreach efforts to inspire women to take on a more active approach in the parenting of their children while teaching them how to create opportunities to explore and achieve their personal and secular goals. Serving in the role of Corporate Public Relations Director for Maryland, Washington DC, and Virginia based companies has allowed Nikia to reach out to audiences and personally impact thousands of lives in the community with educational outreach programs designed to motivate individuals to make positive life changes. "The little lady with the big voice" enjoys motivating through public speaking at seminars, workshops, community, and corporate events.

Coach@amaninicol.com
www.AmaniNicol.com
Tweet @AmaniNicol
Facebook.com/AmaninicolFitness

Boss Lady Basics

Nikia Brown-Sweeney

"Okay ladies now let's get in formation." As those words ring in my ear, surprisingly, I'm not dancing. My mind is envisioning a movement of self-empowerment for women. But this isn't your typical movement made up of thousands of women preparing a historical march. This movement is very personal and the only one in formation is...you! Welcome to Boss Lady Basics, a personal development mini-course designed to transform your next 30 days into a more determined and confident you.

Today is no ordinary day. Before you read any further grab your smartphone, tablet, or journal. Jot down today's date, its significant because it starts your journey to "Boss Lady" status. What is a Boss Lady; a confident, beautiful, positive thinking young woman who takes the CEO position in her life very seriously. Are you a Boss? Do you desire to be a better Boss? Do you feel you have what it takes to carry the Boss Lady mindset into your business...your personal business that is. Have you decided to become the CEO of your life? If you answered yes, then let's move on.

My Now...

During the course of the next 30 days, you'll receive weekly strategies and tips that will improve your positive mindset, healthier outlook on nutrition, and make fitness fun. These strategies along with daily affirmations will strengthen you inside out, physically, and mentally.

It's proven that when we focus on the positive, our outlook changes for the better. Attitude is Altitude! Belief in your abilities, talents, dreams, and goals are critical. Remember you are the CEO of your LIFE. Your vision and your mission are just that...YOURS! Perfect doesn't live here, but putting forth your best effort is never optional.

Are you ready to turn heads and position yourself to accomplish amazing things? Have you realized how unique, beautiful, and unstoppable you really are? And do you know that the successful journey that lies ahead of you is just a page away? Come on girlfriend, let's get started!

During the next 30 days keep a journal. On your calendar schedule weekly Boss Lady Basics (BLB) course time. Monday begins a new week in this course. If your schedule allows, block out an hour on Mondays for the next 4 weeks to consider each strategy and of course, take a few minutes each morning for your daily affirmation. Before we get into our weekly strategies, write down your answers to the following questions:

1. On a scale from 1-10 how would you rate your confidence in your ability to achieve your goals?
2. If you could pick 3 miracles that would make your life even better, what would they be?
3. Whose your role model and why?
4. Imagine you just received an email from a young lady 4 years younger than you. She's writing to tell you how much she values you as her role model. What are her reasons for seeing you as such an example? Write at least three reasons why she looks up to you.

Boss Lady Basics: Week One

Get Healthy Strategy: Go to Bed!

Beauty sleep is not a myth. Sleep has a direct effect on our energy and even weight. After an extended nap, at least that's what I call it when you're sleeping for less than 6 hours, how do you feel in the morning? Even if you have a burst of energy, your body is working off of empty fuel. You're more likely to skip a healthy breakfast, grab a cup of coffee, and an unhealthy snack or food. According to WebMD, "Not only does sleep loss appear to stimulate appetite. It also stimulates cravings for high fat, high carbohydrates foods. Ongoing studies are considering whether adequate sleep should be a standard part of weight loss programs." What's your sleep goal for the week? A good night

My Now...

sleep is 7-9 hours. How many hours of sleep are you committed to getting each night this week?

Boss Lady Fitness: What are you going to do this week to increase your physical activity?

Boss Lady Project: Vision Board. This 3D visual of your goals can be created on poster board, cork board, construction paper, etc. Get creative and have fun. Place your board where you can see it every day. Check out my Vision Board Pins on Amani Nicol's Pinterest.

Affirmations

Monday: I am worthy. I am capable. I am deserving.

Tuesday: I am committed to my own success.

Wednesday: I am beautiful and unique and I embrace all of me.

Thursday: I believe in me and my abilities.

Friday: I am willing to work to get everything I want.

Saturday: I am strong mentally and emotionally.

Sunday: I am cultivating the quality of gratitude because I appreciate the gift of life.

It's the end of your first week, how did you do? Jot it down in your journal.

Boss Lady Basics: Week Two

Get Healthy Strategy: Don't Skip Meals

At times, when we're looking to lose weight, we count calories. Some even attempt to save calories by skipping meals. But this does more harm than good. When a meal is skipped the body becomes deprived of much needed fuel and you lose your natural ability to produce energy. You'll appreciate having more energy throughout your day when you enjoy three healthy meals and snacks in between. Because it's easier to eat unhealthy choices when we're starving, strive to plan ahead by preparing your meals in advance. Cooking at home saves you time, money, and calories. What days of the week could you cook at home? How many days this week will you take a packed lunch and snacks?

Boss Lady Fitness: During last week's workout, did you feel the burn…increase resistance and/or intensity this week?

Boss Lady Project: Write down 3 goals that you would like accomplish this month and place them on the board along with your favorite affirmation.

Affirmations

Monday: I am comfortable asking for what I want because I deserve it.

Tuesday: Everything is possible for me when I set my mind to achieve.

Wednesday: My goals are more than words; they give evidence to my action.

Thursday: Every day is a blessing and I will use it to show appreciation for my Creator.

Friday: Confident, Determined, Motivated, oh yeah, that's me!

Saturday: I am a positive woman with no room for negative talk.

Sunday: I am focused and will not allow anything to waiver my faith in my abilities.

All right now, you're halfway finished the course. How are you doing so far? Were you able to continue following strategies from week one? Write down your results.

Boss Lady Basics: Week Three

Get Healthy Strategy: Eat more "Real" Food

Last week we touched on the importance of 3 balanced meals and snacks in between. This week's strategy will help you make the right food choices. Real foods or "whole foods" are unprocessed or minimally processed. Real foods are nutrient dense with vitamins, minerals, and antioxidants. These foods give us energy and contribute to our overall health. Examples of whole foods are vegetables, fruit, nuts, seeds, legumes, grains, animal protein, and seafood.

What "real" foods can you add to your meals this week?

Boss Lady Fitness: How many days of the week are you working out and how long are your workouts? Remember 3 days a week for at least 30 minutes a day can be very effective. What days, times, and duration of your workout will you accomplish this week?

Boss Lady Project: Allow your creative side to flow. The 3 goals you wrote last week are the foundation to this creative project. Make them come to life with pictures, sayings, drawings, etc.

My Now…

Affirmations

Monday: I am the CEO of my business and therefore will not mind the business of others

Tuesday: I have no reason to envy others, my only competition is me!

Wednesday: I refuse to give into negative emotions; I will use the utmost self-control.

Thursday: I respect my imperfections by being determined to try again and never give up.

Friday: I am inspired to put forth my best and be the best at everything I set out to do.

Saturday: I know my potential. I am not afraid of hard work.

Sunday: I am naturally beautiful inside and out.

It's the end of your third week, how did you do? Jot it down in your journal.

...for the Future Woman

Boss Lady Basics: Week Four

Get Healthy Strategy: Reduce Stress

Let's be real for a moment, when you're the CEO of your Boss Lady Movement, you have a to-do list longer than the day. Balance is necessary. As you set out to accomplish your goals, keep in mind prioritizing tasks while making time for fun and relaxation is important. Feeling stressed can impair digestion, affect hormone levels that can sabotage weight loss efforts and actually cause weight gain. Alright Ms. Boss Lady, how can you reduce your stress level? Can you use time management techniques like prioritizing your tasks? Is scheduled time weekly for me-time possible? Do you have recreation as part of your weekly schedule?

Boss Lady Fitness: Make fitness fun and results will follow. What's your favorite fitness activity? If you love the gym, what's your backup plan if time doesn't allow you to make it during your usual time? How can you make fitness fun and effective with an at home workout?

Boss Lady Project: Now that you've started your vision board, continue to add your personal expressions of your goals, both short term and long term. Remember that what the mind can conceive and constantly see, will be achieved!

My Now...

Affirmations

Monday: I am happy. Happiness starts with me.

Tuesday: I am a go-getter, fear does not define me.

Wednesday: My path is bright and full of possibilities.

Thursday: My best is more than good enough. It's great because I refuse to settle.

Friday: I am working it today!

Saturday: I thrive. I strive. I am rejuvenated.

Sunday: I am taking charge of me. I own it. I am winning.

Wow, time sure does fly. It's the end of your fourth week, how did you do? Jot it down in your journal.

As your Boss Lady Basics Course comes to a close, it's far from over. Continue to use your journal, feel free to repeat the course and if you're ready to take it from Basics to Advance, check out my website for the Advance Boss Lady Course. I hope you are even more confident, relaxed, affirmed, and motivated to accomplish your goals with a winning attitude that draws positive people to you.

> The information provided in this chapter is intended to be helpful, not render medical, health, or any other kind of personal professional services.

...for the Future Woman

My Now...

Donyshia Boston-Hill

Donyshia Boston-Hill is currently the CEO of Keeper of the Brand Marketing and Media Consulting Firm and Ice Princess NYC.

She has held leadership and management positions within several media and entertainment companies, such as HOT 97, 98.7 Kiss FM, 101.9 RXP, The Loud Digital Network, The New York Knicks and Madison Square Garden College Basketball. She has developed a deep relationship with the community activating programs with HOT 97's Hip Hop Has Heart Foundation and the Kiss Cares Foundation. Her vision and creativity was credited for the continuous growth of HOT 97 Summer Jam and the HOT 97 Summer Jam Festival Pre-Event and Attraction from 2002-2014.

Donyshia is an alumna of St. John's University and New York University. She's an active member of Alpha Kappa Alpha, Sorority Incorporated, The Links, Incorporated and Jack and Jill of America, Inc. She is also one of the featured authors of the book, The Fearless Living Experience. She is married to Kevin Boston-Hill and has two lovely children.

Keeperofthebrand.com
Iceprincessnyc.com, Iceprincesscelebrations.com,
IcePrincessLegacy.com
FB: Keeperofthebrand, iceprincesscelebrations, iceprincessweddings
Twitter: @iceprincessnyc, @dbmediamaven, @kotbmarketing
Linkedin: linkedin.com/in/donyshiabenjamin/en
Instagram: @Iceprincessnyc
Pinterest: @Iceprincessnyc

...for the *Future Woman*

Your Living Herstory and Legacy
Donyshia Boston-Hill

"Dearly beloved, we gather here today to get through this thing called life." – Prince

I am honored to share my journey with you as if I were giving advice to my younger self. I hope my words contribute to your growth, so you can build your story and make herstory. Your journey into womanhood is one of the toughest jobs in the world, one you should never experience alone. We'll bid adieu to questionable self-esteem as we navigate a path to greatness and womanhood. I don't pretend to have all the answers but I will try to fill you with real-life advice to help you deal with the pressures of growing up, fitting in and becoming a woman. There are essential tips and strategies every future woman should keep in a lockbox and access during her journey into womanhood for information, inspiration and those ah-ha moments you will have in life. Let's discover and explore why you should love yourself, why smart girls finish on top and the true meaning of friendship. You are worth every word I share because you're a girl, beautiful inside and out, special in different ways and similar in more ways than you may believe.

My Now...

It is generally said that life experiences mold you into the woman you become. My life experiences included being exposed to two worlds. On one hand I grew up in a single parent household with a supportive extended family and father a phone call away, a child of the 80's during a time in New York City when teenage pregnancy was rising, hip hop was becoming a major influence and the war on drugs was a national focus. On the other hand, I was exposed to the arts, played in a marching band and spent several school years in Georgia where I enjoyed the playing in a jazz ensemble. In my youth I happily enjoyed access to activities that most urban city girls don't experience. I have become a Liberal New York City woman, with conservative Georgia values, style and grace. I move at a fast pace but promised myself to step back and enjoy the roses, mentor, and guide everyone around me. Now, that's enough about me.

Let's discover and explore a few tips I've outlined just because you're a Future Woman. Throughout my life I have heard men state, "I'm glad I'm not a girl." I'm here to tell you, you hit the gene pool jackpot. Being a girl is an awesome experience and learning to be a woman is even better.

Have you drafted your 1, 5, 10, or 20 year plans? If not, begin now and remember you will face obstacles and detours along the way. It's how you plan and react to those challenges that will help shape you. Draft away because time waits for no woman. Once that's set, create a list of what steps you need to take to reach your goals. Evaluate how, why and what it will take to get there.

As a woman, we find it hard to ask for help. I want you to know it's ok to raise your hand and ask for guidance. Learn when to ask for help and when to open yourself up for help. You may feel vulnerable but sometimes you need to be pushed towards your next step and into greatness by those that have walked the path you wish to travel.

Secure a Board of Directors

In life you should look at yourself as an investment, a brand and a company. Most companies have a Board of Directors. I recommend you sit quietly and begin drafting a list of mentors that you would assign to your personal Board of Directors. The people on your Board should be a combination of personal mentors and professional mentors. These life coaches and mentors are your go to people when you are unsure about a decision in life. They are also the seasoned people that have traveled the road you're on. They are people that will uplift you by providing guidance. Don't select your best friend just because she's your friend. Select mentors you admire and people that won't just tell you what you want to hear.

- Research Formal Mentorship Programs

- Utilize Digital and Social Media to connect with Prospective Mentors
    - Email and request 15 Minutes of their time for advice
    - Connect on LinkedIn, Twitter, Facebook
    - Call their office and schedule an interview
    - Send a written request

Interview potential board members without their knowledge. Ask question about their life, career path and how they achieved their level of success or overcame difficult times.

Insider tip: People love talking about themselves.

Self Esteem

Fitting in and being comfortable in your own skin takes years of practice. I have observed many women with low self-esteem and it truly saddens me. In my opinion, low self-esteem turns young ladies into angry women and no one likes an angry woman.

Don't worry, you have been fitting in since you were born so you have years of practice. When facing first impressions - head up, shoulders back, deep breath, inhale, exhale and smile. Add a confident walk and overcome fear. When all else fails – SMILE. It is true a smile can change the way you feel and the way others view you. Quickly try smiling and think about your happy place. I hope your smile gave you a warm feeling inside.

How would you rate your self-esteem level? If you're not sure, I've outlined a few signs of low self-esteem to watch out for:

- Wishing you were someone else
- Feeling unworthy or inferior
- Thinking you're not smart enough
- Thinking you're not pretty enough
- Thinking you're not talented enough
- Feeling you're not good enough

Let's boost your self-esteem with these exercises:

1. Look in the mirror and say,
   a. Hello gorgeous
   b. I love you
   c. Yes, I'm beautiful inside and out
2. Dance around the house and say, "I'm working hard and I will be successful".
3. Change your conversation with your family, friends and peers: Ask them to tell you something good; something new; something you don't know about them.

My Now...

Now let's try this Self Esteem Mad Lib: Fill in the blanks

Hello Beautiful!

Yes _____, I'm talking to you.
     (Your name here)

You are a future woman, one of the greatest inventions since _____.
     (insert an invention prior to your birth year)

You are amazing and I love when you _____.
                                      (verb/talent/hobbies)

Today is the last day you will dwell on being _____ _____
                                                (negative adjective)   (Body Image – you don't like)
and _____.
     (Embarrassing thing you did or Mistake you made)

You're going to start loving yourself for being _____, _____ and _____.
                                                 (positive adjective)   (positive adjective)   (positive adjective)

So, _____ because you are the _____-est woman on earth.
     (favorite endearment)   (positive adjective)

More precious than a flawless diamond.

...for the Future Woman

Body Image

You were born with the DNA given to you by your parents, it's your responsibility to love the skin you're in and take care of your body. We transition from girl to woman with the effects of puberty. You will experience changes and it's normal. Don't compare yourself to Famous / Celebrity people or peers. Exercise at every age matters. Even if you take just 25 minutes a day for yourself you will feel the difference and see the difference over time. If you take care of your body, it will take care of you. Yes, your body is your temple and the only body you have. I wore braces for years and my retainer is my best friend. If you are truly unhappy with a body part, seek guidance and help from your Board of Directors. Shy away from trends, what's cool today will be out dated tomorrow. A hairstyle can be easily updated, however plastic surgery, although it's becoming the new normal, is a major decision that should not be taken lightly.

Friendship

As girls and women, we love having friends. The hard part is learning how to be a good friend and evaluating levels of friendship. I'm sure you have friends that are the only people in life that truly understand you. You have spent hours together via phone, text, social media, and at events. They are the people that know you through the good times, the bad times and your secrets. You will have different levels of friendships: BFF's, acquaintances, colleagues and digital friends to name a few.

Here are a few tips about friendship as you transition through life:

1. Surround yourself with people that have similar goals and aspire for more.
2. Take time to get to know your friends and their attributes. They should be trustworthy, like-minded, positive, and forward thinking.
3. Everyone is not your friend. I'm sure you heard that before but it's true. Friends realize that you're not perfect.
4. You should be able to tell your friends you care about them, I'm sorry when you make a mistake, and always be forgiving.
5. Stay away from clicks, "frenemies" and build your circle of trust.
6. There will come a time when you are not able to connect with your friends daily - true friendship stands the test of time and distance.

Most importantly, have fun with your friends and create memories. As your life changes, your friendships will change which is fine as long as you're true to all parties and yourself.

Growing Up

Becoming a woman is an amazing life experience. You are going to make mistakes but the key to your success is learning from those mistakes. That's how you grow. If you find yourself on the merry-go-round of life repeating bad habits, check yourself. Yes, check yourself. It's always great to receive feedback from others but your inner voice and self-approval can also come from within. Inside you know when you are making the right decision or a major mistake. As women we have an inner voice, that intuition and instinct that will help us in times of need. This road called life will have many twist and turns, good times and bad, but don't allow fear to control fate. ALWAYS give 110% of your efforts in everything you do and you will finish on top.

In closing, it's our responsibility as women to instill confidence in you. You're a valued member of society and I leave you with this acronym to keep in mind:

F.U.T.U.R.E W.O.M.A.N:

F: FIRST Impressions say a lot to people about you and vice versa. Always put your best foot forward. On the other side, don't be quick to judge people when you first meet them. Everyone has a story.

U: Women are different and being different is what makes you UNIQUE and special.

T: TRUST in your gut instinct. Seek advice from your board of directors.

U: UNDERSTANDING makes you better. Always ask questions that will give you clarity on the UGLY things in life.

R: Growth is not immediately REACTING to every situation. Sometimes sitting back and learning to be objective will garner the results you want to achieve.

E: Being EARLY is always better than being on time or late. It shows your dedication to the task and sends the message that you are efficient.

...for the Future Woman

W: <u>W</u>ARMTH and kindness will take you further in life than being a mean girl. Kindness does not mean weakness. It makes you invaluable.

O: Live life on the <u>O</u>FFENSE instead of the defense. Create a list of your goals and outline what you need to accomplish to obtain your goals. Then stick to your plan.

M: <u>M</u>en will always be there. Date, enjoy life and put yourself and dreams first. Mr. Right will come along and your relationship will be easy.

A: A positive <u>A</u>ttitude will bring good things to your life.

N: <u>N</u>ever forget the lessons you learn in life. The lessons you learn in life will be your foundation for future decisions.

If you follow your plan, map out your journey and stick to the plan you will make HERSTORY. Your plan will build the foundation for your personal and professional legacy. As a woman, you want to leave a positive footprint on the world. Please allow the Future Women to become your inner voice as you travel through life. Feel free to share these positive words with other women around you because giving back is fulfilling.

My Now...

In the future, I hope you pay forward buy sharing your wisdom with Future Women. Now, aren't you glad you were born a GIRL?

...for the Future Woman

Part 3: My Now

My Now...

Fallon Lewis

Fallon Lewis hails from Decatur, GA and is a very proud woman who has accomplished many great things so far in life. Receiving two wonderful degrees, awards and many recognitions are a few highlights but starting her own business iNspire GEMS LLC has been her greatest accomplishment yet. Instead of being the victim of life situations, Fallon used those moments as her motivation for growth and to show others guidance in becoming who they are meant to be. With the wisdom and knowledge gained Ms. Lewis started speaking to youth and young adults about healthy relationships in a fun, innovative and life changing way. As Fallon continues to walk in her purpose she is very humble and grateful to God for the ability to continually thrive in what she was created to do. Fallon Lewis is a true Gem and she has arrived, will you please take a moment and welcome her!!

Website: www.speakfae.com
Email:info@speakfae.com
Instagram:@thatsfae

...for the Future Woman

Why Now and Not Then?
Fallon Lewis

That's a great question one asks when you are sitting and listening to a complete stranger tell you about your life and explaining why you act, feel, and have dealt with the unnecessary people and things in life. With no movement like a statue my body sat still and my mind went through every situation I could think of and just that fast, all of the wrong that was pushed deep down had now resurfaced and having a front seat in my life. The only thing missing was a bowl of popcorn. I didn't know for sure how this small yet major moment was going to change my life but I knew it was going to be uncomfortable and I was ready for the challenge.

My life was very good as a child. I enjoyed school, made good grades and was just an overall great kid. I grew up in a single parent home with my mother and siblings. I was familiar with my dad but never had the guidance I needed from him. As a teen there were times I wanted him around but reality showed me otherwise. Eventually I saw it was a blessing in disguise which I finally understood many years later. Nonetheless I made decisions, especially ones towards guys the best way I knew how to which was going by what my friends were saying or what I thought was right. Around the time I reached puberty I started to feel indifferent about my blemishes. Nobody ever picked on me it was just a personal issue that I had within myself and I wanted it fixed. It was awkward sometimes because there were other female students who didn't have many blemishes or have as much as myself. Not fair at all, so I thought and at that moment I became self-conscious of my face which led me to wearing makeup trying to hide what I didn't want others to see. As time progresses, during my high school years I become more in tune with having a nice shape and my one of a kind personality so much that I didn't focus so much on my blemishes. They took a backseat and now I am hearing how pretty, funny and beautiful I was from my peers and in return each day I walked more in confidence simply being myself.

I had a different family, a good one but different. We didn't affirm each other on a regular and that might have played a part of my self-conscious issue too. Good communication was also not a strong component within my family. When it came to values I knew mostly about them from going to church and being rooted in God. I knew what the bible spoke of, heard it taught and preached from Pastors but didn't hear some of those things explained the "real" way at home. My mother didn't sit down and talk about sex or saving yourself and explain the reasons why. It was almost as if it was a given to know what I shouldn't do therefore she didn't have to say much because there were expectations in place. I remember at times while riding in the car with my mom she would say things like "don't sit with your legs open" or "close your legs up". I knew why she said it but I wanted her to spit it out and just say why I shouldn't. Aaaaaahhh!!! I don't have any resentment of the lack of explanations because I realized most of the time people are only able to transfer the things they were taught. If she didn't know, how could she properly tell me any other way? Consequently, I roughed relationships and friendships out through trial and error and sometimes it was very painful and confusing. I learned to cope and just patch the problems up instead of actually finding a solution. I wasn't willing to communicate and if I did it was definitely the wrong way. When I left off for college I told myself I was going to change and become a better person for myself and that's what I thought I did but reality hit me again.

College years were some of my favorite years. I shared a lot of time laughing, learning and making friends with people from many different places. I recall one day on campus people were hugging me left and right and I began to feel uneasy because I thought they wanted something from me. That was an awful mindset I had but that's my truth. I was living a good life in college but it was so uncomfortable at the same time. I graduated college and finished graduate school over the next few years and I was beyond excited with 2 degrees under my belt but something was still missing. Relationships weren't on a positive note due to failing at them for reasons such as stubbornness and poor

My Now...

communication. I also didn't know if I was ready to give all of myself to just one person forever. I saw too many failed marriages and even though I wanted to be married I knew that was something I was not working towards right then. So I became very independent in doing things my way, saying what I wanted to say and doing whatever I wanted that by the time a real relationship was on the rise I was in trouble and stuck in my ways. I had walls up, didn't trust people, wondering if they had a motive, questioned why they like me or why do they like me now. So many things ran through my head. I know I pointed the finger and found fault in them more than I did within myself until that one day, the words coming from a stranger would open the great, effective door to something really good. At the age of 27 the words I heard made me realize the beautiful and valuable woman I had been all along and at that moment I knew the "real me" was pushing its way back out and there was no turning back.

The "stranger" became one of the greatest influences of my life! She made me jot down things about myself and revisit ugly memories only to get me to love all of me from the inside out. The training I was attending focused on healthy relationships and automatically I went in with a mindset of boyfriend and girlfriend, husband and wife but I was so wrong. To allow a healthy relationship to form one must first begin with understanding yourself better. When you have identified those things within yourself you are now able to be the ultimate prize to yourself and whom you are with. With that being said I had to dig and face my ugly, hurtful, disappointing past in front of all of these other adults. It was mind blowing how much of a mess I was based off what I allowed to enter my mind from loved ones and close friends. The knowledge I was receiving had my soul on fire. Each time we did an activity or talked as a group I was quiet, trying to take it all in because I was determined to not ever beat myself up again in regards to who I am. I wouldn't dare be in a dysfunctional relationship or friendship with people again. If someone was broken, I was going to show them the way and help them to get the deep and hidden issue out. No other woman could tell me I wasn't pretty or good enough because I knew my worth. I was empowered! After leaving that training I reflected for a very long time about past relationships with family, friends and boyfriends and I remember saying out loud to myself "why didn't anyone ever tell me this?" I felt cheated. That question right there was heavy on my heart and mind so much because if I had known some of the things I learned that day I would have made better choices and had the self-esteem I needed and longed for a long time ago. All those years of living life but not living it to its full capacity made me wipe my tears, erase all doubt and move forward with a boldness like never before. It wasn't an easy journey to start but it was worth it and benefited me so much. God's love and grace lifted me and kept me going.

After a year of repairing myself I got into a relationship and I was really ready for it because I learned the right way to love myself therefore I knew how I was to love and value him.

Growing in love together and showing him how to correct the past in his life has benefited and blessed our relationship so much. It's not a perfect relationship but it is an awesome relationship. I have to credit him in helping me in continuing to become the great and marvelous woman I am today. His words of encouragement, patience, and loving my flaws and all allowed me to gain emotional strength and power like never before. I remember a road trip to the beach and I just so happen to have an attitude because I am a big planner and like to stick to a schedule and we were late. We arrived to the beach and the minute we get there the sun went away and stormy clouds hovered over. I started to feel sad because I thought the trip was ruined. We got out the car anyway and sat down on the sand as many people started to walk the opposite direction to their cars. We talked with the fresh air blowing and the sound of the waves were in the background. Of all moments I have a revelation about myself that I had to speak on right then and let it "blow in the wind". I began to share with him that as a child I recall my dad saying what he was going to do such as send us things and it never happened. I now saw that the stubbornness and attitude I was displaying at that moment wasn't meant for my boyfriend but it was the anger and resentment I had towards my dad who didn't keep his word. I thought that I didn't have an issue with my dad being in my life but in this case I was wrong. Funny how a man who I wasn't around majority of my life played a heavy part in my actions towards self and others. I saw that at 29 years old I was going back to the disappointed little girl and those past feelings were being shown vividly in the present. Wow! I was shocked yet relieved. As a man he apologized for my dad and spoke some great things into me but one thing he said that stood out the most was "Things in life happen for a reason. Your dad may not have known any better so forgive him. It's up to you to be powerful or pitiful about the situation. Which one will you be?" Those words ushered us into the car as the storm arrived and even though there was a physical storm taking place, my personal storm had passed over and the sun was shining bright.

Now I am at a place of peace within and loving everyone even through their mess because I once was in the same shoes. They say hindsight is perfect sight and the things I learned allowed me to start my own business to help people build healthy relationships within themselves and those they are connected with. There are some days when I may experience a lack of love and on those days I turn away from negative sources and go to my source of strength to clear my mind and get back to the basics of what matters. All of the pain, hurt, nonsense, doubt and many other words to describe what I experienced was preparation for my destiny. I have a greater appreciation and understand that what I complained about could've been worse. When a person says hateful and nasty things about my appearance, judge me off of material objects or try to destroy my character, I simply laugh because I absolutely love the skin I am in and I know who I am. I am Love, Confidence, Strength, Ambition, Bold, Success,

My Now…

Peace, Joy, Abundance and I am Grateful!! I recognize that beauty and love for tangible things doesn't make you do anything but stay in constant search of self. It's the intangible things that keep you positively moving forward. No longer do I take it personal when people see things in me that they are longing for themselves. It only confirms that we all have work to do to help the next woman to freely blossom. Purging and facing the ugly truth broke down walls and barriers that kept me in bondage too long. I saw that I was a pearl of great price and allowed my imperfections to mold me into the perfect treasure. One of the many quotes I live by daily is from Rumi which says "Yesterday I was clever so I wanted to change the world. Today I am wise so I am changing myself". I realized that the more I change myself and evolve into this beautiful black butterfly, what I possess will naturally leap over into those I encounter and the world will be changed effortlessly. What happen THEN manifested the great things NOW. I found my purpose and I am following His.

...for the Future Woman

Stacie Whitaker-Harris

Stacie J. Whitaker-Harris, is a Minister of the Gospel; blessed to share gifts as an Author, Poet, Vocalist and Inspirationalist. She is an Advocate for Social Equality; holding a Bachelor of Arts in Nonprofit Management from the University of Baltimore and currently pursuing a Master of Arts in Law at Regent University.

Stacie is the author of "Hell & Heaven at 8", co-author of the "Whitaker Book of Poetry", contributing author of "My Now for the College Grad", prior freelance writer for the Baltimore Examiners Faith and Culture column and visionary for the Embracing me blog which shares uplifting messages with over 60 countries.

Whitaker's deep compassion, great faith, and resilient spirit continuously allows her to overcome life's challenges thereby inspiring everyone she encounters. She is the loving mother of three Jewels who believes in fortifying the foundation of families for the betterment of mankind.

Website: www.2embraceme.com
Email: GodsGiftLLC@gmail.com

...for the Future Woman

Not Tomorrow

Stacie Whitaker-Harris

"Don't put off until tomorrow what you can do today."
Benjamin Franklin

Tick-tock, the clock strikes one. Tick-tock, tick-tock, tick-tock, tick-tock. Time spins out of control and we feel an ever pressing urgency to follow the spin of the clock, spinning in like manner instead of setting the pace by which time moves around and ultimately for us. We either over-estimate time, under estimate time, try desperately to forget time, or move frantically to the tick of the clock through time.

Initially, my goal was to share what I have learned as a woman, mother, student, minister and entrepreneur regarding time management. However, while preparing my contribution to this project, I realized *Not Tomorrow* also represents a journey **IN TIME** for the development of every aspect of who we are and who we are becoming as women.

Last year I found myself pondering my life's progression. Really, my thoughts leaned more towards a lack of progression.

My Now...

I gauged my success and accomplishments on an invisible compass called time. Why? Because 2015 marked an exciting milestone in my life (My 40th Birthday). I should have been ecstatic about this life event, especially after several near death experiences. Instead, I grappled with being single, not having my own home, not completing my education in what I thought was a timely manner, a failed business, incomplete personal and professional projects, and even the fact that I made multiple mistakes over the course of my thirty-nine years of life.

How often have you heard people use these or similar phrases:

"Yesterday's the past, tomorrow's the future, but today is a gift."

"Better three hours too soon than a minute too late."

"How did it get so late so soon."

"Time waits for no one."

"The race is not given to the swift but to the one who endures until the end."

These frequently used quotes by Dr. Seuss, William Shakespeare, Bil Keane and others, all speak an undeniable truth; everyone focuses on time at some point in life. For me, I thought about how much time I wasted chasing love, hunting money, looking for success, or simply being fearful to act due to prior false steps.

My reminiscent reflections took me back to when I was a pregnant high school teen. One teacher tried to convince me that I would never complete anything in life because I chose to keep my baby. This same teacher provided false information so I would leave my prestigious high school to attend a school for pregnant teenagers. She assured me I would be readmitted to my school once the baby was born. However, she left out the fact that the pregnant school's curriculum did not match that of my high school and thus, I would not be reconsidered for admittance. With a little research and the assistance of another teacher, I stayed at my school. Although I did not walk across the stage with my classmates due to health issues, I did obtain my high school diploma June 1994 just like everyone else. Shortly after graduation all my friends went off to college while I worked two, sometimes three jobs to care for my child. Three years after graduation I found myself married with two children. I was rather upset with myself as my friends were either graduating from college or preparing to graduate. I figured I messed up my chances of going to college when I got pregnant in high school. My job at the bank was rewarding, but simply not enough. My cousin explained how I could attend college and so I did.

My mind went on to consider how I spent more than seven years in junior college and an additional five years seeking a

My Now...

Bachelor's degree. By the time I graduated most of my high school friends had completed Master's and even Doctoral degrees. They were just beginning to settle down, purchase homes, and start families. On the other hand, I was divorced but preparing to remarry; in the process of purchasing my first home and then suddenly going through foreclosure; attending graduate school one minute and flunking out the next; breaking up with my fiancée and suddenly losing everything (including my dignity, pride, some friends and family members). Yes, seems everything happened all at once and I felt stuck in the downward spiral of a time warp. I spent the next couple of years frustrated, depressed, and afraid to make decisions for fear of making the wrong decisions, which further exacerbated the depression and slowed my overall progress in reaching my goals.

After many trials and through multiple errors, I learned:

1. There is NO such thing as a faulty timeline
2. Time is adjustable, flexible, and fluid in the mind of the one who is optimistic
3. Past times do not possess the power to stifle movement in current times
4. Procrastination is not the only way to waste time - Wrestling with your thoughts is the greatest manipulator of time
5. Do not set a permanent life clock because sometimes clocks break so be willing to reset

6. Live life one moment at a time and trust that time is working in your favor

And much more. Remember, your success is not predicated on the timeline of others.

Failure only gains strength when you settle at defeats doorstep. In other words, when you stop simply because you "failed" or you did not acquire your desired outcome the first time, your mind determines your failures. Learn and grow from them and allow your failures to lead you to the road of multiple successes.

As you grow throughout the course of life, consider completing a semi-annual self-assessment. Although not a comprehensive list, ask yourself the following:

1. What type of woman am I and how have I grown?
2. Does time have me spinning out of control or am I using time to my advantage?
3. What have I done to facilitate spiritual, mental, physical, and financial growth?
4. Have I accomplished goals set previously? If not, what am I doing to achieve my goals?
5. Do I allow everyday problems and issues to toss me to and fro? If yes, what do I need to do to stop this process?

6. Who am I surrounded by and do these people encourage growth and development?
7. Are my relationships healthy and do I set clear boundaries? (Relationships can be with family members, friends, co-workers, business partners, etc.)
8. Am I powerfully and positively impacting the lives of those I encounter?
9. Do I take time for myself daily, weekly, or monthly to regenerate?
10. Ultimately, am I happy with where I am currently? If not, what do I need to do to change?

All in all remember that greatness is NOW, in every moment, every day, so be your best self TODAY -- NOT TOMORROW!

Develop your mind. Develop your weaknesses. Develop your ability to push through difficulties. Develop consistency! Develop, Develop, Develop! The keys to your success are in your hands; it's all just a matter of continuance so utilize time to your advantage.

...for the Future Woman

A few quotes from Author Stacie J. Whitaker-Harris

Do not look back, or down, nor up for too long; focus on what is currently in front of you while aspiring to reach beyond

You can't unknow what you know, but you can unlearn thoughts and behaviors you learned

Working to repair what's broken, yields euphoric results which in turn renders growth, development, and the type of lifestyle you once dreamed of

The mind can be your best friend or your worst enemy.

Perception is everything and nothing at all!

When you know the truth but choose to continue to live according to its opposite you live a contradiction because you choose to and not because the truth is hidden. Therefore, YOU have created your own false life. Be authentic with yourself first!

The greatest vindication is not seeking revenge, but instead, living your best life.   Now that is vindication at its finest!

LIKE A PRISONER

In a cage of heavy metal and concrete

No room to move just thoughts of defeat

Ice cold gray bars of steel

Speaking aloud, this just can't be real

Thick clouds of darkness no kiss from the sun

Now you're thinking back, what have I done

Teeth like fangs, the only light shown

Back against the wall, am I really alone

Sounds of deep breathing are growing loud

Realizing now there's a huge crowd

So many others in the room too

There out to get me, what will I do

Knees bent, eyes filled with tears

In the darkness I exude my deepest fears

Nowhere to run as the walls close in

...for the Future Woman

I see their faces, small teeth, slight grin

I search for an exit but not one could I find

Thoughts and regrets flood my mind

Struggling to breathe, gasping for air

Senses alert, ahead do I stare

Seeking to regain freedom, break free from pain

Bulging blood vessels, my hearts under strain

Enslaved by thoughts, my mind runs wild

Reverting to youth, my days as a child

Overwhelmed I blurt out my deepest confession

Bells ring, I snap out of my daily session

Realizing now it's all a matter of thought

This daily battle again must be fought

The fight between them, those, him, and her

Again, in my mind, I'm my own prisoner

My Now…

Tonya Parker

Tonya's the Founder of Trailblazers International, with over 15 years of experience as a Mentor to women of all ages, and from all walks of life.

She assist ministry teams across the nation; and has played an instrumental part in the strategic planning and implementation of major conferences, and community enrichment events. Tonya brings extensive practical, and tactical solutions to the table, as well as leadership guidance.
As a Federal Employee, she's traveled both stateside and abroad; however, it is Trailblazers that affords her the opportunity to meet, and touch the lives of many by encouraging, motivating and pressing them to their ordained place in destiny.

She host of Moments in Destiny, Ladies Night Out; an evening of Real, But Right Talk, for women 18 and over. She also hosts Prophetic Roundtable Discussions; on Building an Apostolic & Prophetic Culture, Resulting in Kingdom Growth.

Contact info: www.TrailblazersIntl.org
TParker@TrailblazersIntl.org
https://www.facebook.com/TrailblazersInternational
https://instagram.com/trailblazersintl/

...for the Future Woman

Can't Stop Now, Destiny is Calling
Tonya Parker

Recently, I had the honor of being asked to minister during a women's conference, where the theme was "Women Advancing the Kingdom of Heaven; Through Releasing, Embracing, and Conquering". It was shortly thereafter, I did what I always do after an assignment, and I continued to ponder the theme. It was then that the question came to mind, "Did I share everything with them, or what else could I have told someone like them, seeking to advance in Destiny?" What else could I have said that would cause them to make an impact forever? Well, the answer was very simple, but yet profound. The answer was that we all need to learn how to guard against the spirit of hesitation and give God a complete yes!

You see for many of us, it's not that God has not destined greatness for us; but often times, we tend to fall prey to the spirit of hesitation which causes delay or even abortion in our spiritual lives. You see, we must understand that whenever we're presented with an opportunity to move to a higher place, or higher dimension in God; we simply cannot afford to hesitate.

My Now...

Whenever we are presented with an opportunity to move to a higher place, or a higher dimension, whether that's in seeking education, going after that promotion, pursuing that possibility of marriage, properly managing our finances, our businesses, and yes, even our relationship in God, the unknown can be fearful, and hesitation will always try to grip us. What I've found is that hesitation seems to always present itself in an array of excuses, especially within the church. You find yourself saying "Well, I'm just being cautious, I'm being prayerful, or I'm counting up the cost. So, in fact, I'm actually using wisdom before moving out into anything new; doing due diligence". While that's a very valid and noteworthy response, and I do believe that we all should practice prudence in any decision making process, I still believe that we must guard against the spirit that causes us to overthink, and over process, to the point that it begins to paralyze us and keeps us from moving forward.

There have been many days that I've had to stop and say to my husband, "I see where our son gets it from, because the truth is, you're so smart, so intelligent, and you have your college degree, and with all of that, it's paralyzed you in some ways. You have a tendency to overthink things and make them much harder than God really intended for them to be". You see, our son, though extremely intelligent, always on the honor roll and graduated with advanced studies, always had the problem with overthinking assignments. There were many days his teachers would say to him, "What took you so long to get to the end? You had the answer, you worked the problem out just like you should have, but you began to second guess yourself, and overthink the situation, and thus did more work than was necessary".

And similarly, in the Kingdom of God, we tend to make things far more complicated than they really have to be. We become so anxious with matters of timing, that we tend to miss the significance of the opportunity that the times represent. This is why when the disciples asked Jesus in Acts 1:6-7, "at what time will the Kingdom of Heaven be restored?" He said it's not for you to "know the times nor the seasons", because time is under His authority. When God is ready for us to step into our next place in destiny, our assignment is simply to walk through the door, whenever the door is opened.

You see, as women moving forward, it's not just enough for us to have faith, but we've got to ACT in faith. We must be careful that we don't become so preoccupied with actual minutes and seconds on the clock, that we fail to realize and miss our appointed time, our moment of opportunity, and yes, even our due season that God has designed just for us!

This is why we must learn to say yes quickly to the Lord; because when we delay, hesitation can cause us to end up missing God's divine placement for our lives. If we're honest and begin to take a look back over our shoulders, we can clearly see today, that is really what delayed us last year, or even the year before that. You see, oftentimes we allow coward-ness to masquerade as caution; because we become afraid of how big the opportunity is that's before us.

And when that happens, we tend to use cute little Christian clichés to buy us time, such as "let me take it to God in prayer", when actually God is saying, "Why are you bringing it back to me? I'm the one that gave you the mandate to move forward in the first place?" And so, as a result, hesitation causes us to almost miss our destination! But this is the season that you simply cannot allow this to happen. How do you do that? By walking thru every door that God opens for you. If He opens it, now is the time to walk through it.

You break every form of hesitation in your life, simply by walking through the door, by applying for every opportunity that presents itself to you. You my sister must make yourself available for everything that God has for you. It's time that you maximize every Godly moment that He brings before you. Now is the time to pursue every possibility that He's set before you.

For many, our lives become stagnated because we find ourselves wrestling between two opinions; which is what the spirit of hesitation will do to you. James 1:8 states that a double minded man is unstable in all of his ways. When you are unstable in your mind, you become indecisive in your thoughts; and when you are indecisive in your thoughts, you become stuck in your life. You my sister must declare that your stuck days are indeed over; and it's time for you to get to your expected end. You see, you must learn to take a righteous risk for your future and trust God for your righteous reward.

Certainly, there have been days that we felt that we've been in this place long enough. Well, this is the season that God desires to take the brakes off; and you must agree with Him by answering your call into the ministry, to go back to school, to start that business, or even to buy that house, or car. Yes, it's time to respond to that which you hear God speaking into your heart. Truth of the matter is that you can't afford to hesitate any longer, because this next move is not just about you. It's about the next generation that is coming behind you.

In Numbers 13, we see that like many of you, the time had come for the children of Israel to shift to their new place in destiny and possess all of the things that God had promised them. Yes, this special group of people had entered into a season where God was ready to transition them from one place in destiny to the next. Likewise, with many of you, this place in which God was calling them to walk into was a land of great promise. It was symbolic of salvation, sanctification, and God's sovereign covenant with His people. God was saying to them, as He's saying to you even today, "I know that you've had a long journey, but I've prepared a place just for you"; even in the presence of your enemies, but you simply cannot hesitate to possess it.

You see, as you defeat the spirit of hesitation, and give a complete yes to God, He is going to release redemption for your life. Like He did for the children of Israel, it is God's desire to graduate you into a season of relief, refreshment, rescue, and a season of rest.

God was about to put an end to their season of mediocrity; and move them into a season of productivity. As you confront the spirit of hesitation, you will begin experiencing God moving you into a season of not just fertility, but fruitfulness; a season of more than enough.

What God has in store for you is a place of abundance; it's a place that is overflowing with milk and honey. This new place is a new way of life; it's a place that God will put an end to your years of wandering without purpose and call your destiny into being. However, in order to graduate to your next place in destiny; and into another realm of faith in God, you must be discerning enough to know timing! Time is everything, and it's also the one thing that you can't afford to waste. Walking into your new season means that you must apprehend, arrest, and lay hold of every opportunity that God sets before you, in spite of the obstacles that are happening around you. Stepping in simply means taking advantage of what God has divinely orchestrated on your behalf, in order to put you in position today to have the best victory and success for your tomorrow.

You see, after sufficient time of evaluation and observation in spying out the land of Canaan, there were those who were connected to them that came back and said we've seen the abundance, we've seen the land, and it is indeed, one that is overflowing with milk and honey. But that's not all that's in the land, there are some giants there; and the cities are fortified and the bible says that THEY concluded that they were fine right where they were, and wouldn't apprehend their next season of opportunity.

Did you see that? It was theirs, God had destined it for them; and here they were looking at the place, seeing the promises ready to manifest in their lives, but afraid to take possession because of what it looked like, and the possibility of a fight.

Listen, when God has destined something for your life, it doesn't matter what the things around you look like. The presence of the enemy does not negate, nor does it nullify the promises of God for your life. Just because there are some other people holding it doesn't mean that you still can't have it. No, not at all, because like you, I had to discover that what God has for me, it is for me. Just because it's in someone else's possession does not mean that it's not mine. It's still your promise, because the wealth of the wicked is reserved for the righteous. (Proverbs 13:22)

All you need to know is that God already has a blessing with your name on it. I know that there are some giants occupying the promise, but sometimes God will entrust temporary custody of your blessings, not so that another person can stay there, but simply so they can maintain it, and take care of it until you get there. No, He doesn't mean for them to stay there, but He intends for them to steward your promise.

After all, how do you think the grapes and the pomegranates were so big and luscious? God put them in place to protect and nurture the promise that He had set aside just for them. And like you, God had them there to cultivate and farm it. He did all of that so that by the time you arrived, you could reap what you did not sow; and eat, what you did not plant, and live in and what you did not build. (Deut 6:11)

Like us oftentimes, they were intimidated by the fact that the land was already occupied, and couldn't envision stepping into their new season. They had issues seeing themselves beyond their present day circumstances, which caused them to back up and doubt what God said. I understand life can be rough at times, yet as Believers, we must never forget that our God is not only a promise maker, but He is a promise keeper. The enemy of our soul knows that he can't stop your blessings, so he tries to damage how you see yourself in relation to the blessing. He uses every wicked way in his arsenal, to keep us from maximizing our faith and becoming overcomers thru Christ Jesus our Lord. (Romans 8:37)

The enemy has no problem using anxiety, depression, fear, and all kinds of assaults on our minds, and against your self-worth. He doesn't mind attacking your self-esteem, his ammo is to always come against your confidence, and dare I even say your confidence even in our God.

And what's unfortunate is that oftentimes, we cooperate with the enemy's distorted view of us, because we look at the strength of the giants versus the strength of our God. And whenever you lift up a man's attributes higher than you lift the authority of God's Word, you will always see yourself as inferior and inadequate. You see, a damaged perception of self, is one of the worse crimes that you could ever put on yourself. Your inability to see yourself as God sees you will rob you of the blessings that God has destined for you.

Not recognizing or knowing your own self-worth, or your own value in God will always cause you to live an unfulfilled, unfruitful and unfaithful life. This is why it's imperative that you understand that even though the enemy has tried his best to intimidate you, and make you feel smaller than; and less than, by embarrassing you out of your new season, you've come to a place that you understand that it's time to give God a complete yes and move forward, in spite of.

Now giving God a complete yes, and moving into your promise means that some days will be harder than others. Though possible, it will be difficult, because you will be forced to deal with the mentality, education, connections of a grasshopper, and even the looks of a grasshopper, Yes, God has you on the cusp of promotion, but you still must be careful that you don't commit self-sabotage because of a broken identity of self.

You see often times we frame our identity in the context of the relationships that we possess. However, it's when I possess a sober assessment of myself, not in relationship to my job, but in relationship to my God, that I'm able to see that I already have the victory. You simply must tap into greater pursuit, greater praise, greater possibility, and yes, the greater anointing to do what He has destined only you to do.

And so, when we look at it in this frame, perhaps the real obstacle that oftentimes stands in our way isn't the enemy, but it's the INNER ME. Let me help you today, you will never conqueror your external giants, until you gain the courage to confront your internal grasshopper. You see once you release the grasshopper mentality, and get a God view for your life, then and only then does it not matter how you look to anyone else. The only thing that matters is how you look to God.

This is why you've got to be ok with who you were created to be! We can't lose any more hair, gain another pound, nor lose any more sleep wondering how other people see us. God wants to set you free from the opinions of other people; and who the Son sets free is free indeed! (John 8:36) People didn't die for you, they didn't suffer for you, they didn't call you, they can't heal you; so instead of wondering how you look in everybody else's eyes, and you've got to fix your eyes on Jesus, who is the author and the finisher of your faith. (Heb 12:2)

Let me leave you with this, when you're making a destiny decision, it's not enough to get a majority report. Sometimes you've got to go back and get a second opinion and that's what Caleb did. Caleb said I could care less what they are saying; at the end of the day, I still believe that we are still able to overcome. While others were focused on the giants, Caleb was focused on the grapes; because when there is an anointing on your life for more, you don't see yourself as a victim, but you see yourself as victorious.

When there is a special grace that covers you, there are three things that must take place as every season approaches:

1. You cannot hesitate to trust God with the next step.

2. You cannot stay connected with people that only want to observe, when God has called you to occupy.

3. You must come into agreement with what God says for your life; by giving Him a complete yes, every step of the way, even when you don't understand.

Caleb said, we are well able, and guess what? So are you, after all, there is a place in destiny that's calling your name.

...for the Future Woman

Sharon A. Myers

Sharon A. Myers is the Founder and CEO of Moovin4ward Presentations, an empowerment company that facilitates leadership development, and entrepreneurial programs for youth, students and professionals. She is the developer of several youth programs to include Journey to Success: Personal Success Strategic Plan (PSSP) Program, which is based on the book Mapping Your Journey to Success: Six Steps for Personal Planning. She has also developed the My Now Career & Leadership Conference and the Young Entrepreneur Success (YES!) Program.

sharon@moovin4ward.com
www.Moovin4ward.com
www.Moovin4wardTraining.com
www.Journey2SuccessPSSP.com
www.MyNowBooks.com
Tweet @moovin4ward

...for the Future Woman

@MyPrincess #URRoyalty

Sharon A. Myers

#WhoYouAre

You are a princess. You come from royalty. You represent royalty. And one day, you'll be a Royal Queen.

Your father is a formidable and valiant King, and your mother is a majestic and fearless Queen. Both are children of God, the creator of your royal heritage.

You are a princess. Not because your parents are wealthy, because they aren't. But you do possess far more than your parents ever had. I'm not speaking of material things, but of access to options that didn't exist for the generations before you. You have access to a wealth of knowledge, tools to learn, and resources to achieve your dreams. There are no limits. There are no excuses.

You are a princess. Not because of the color of your skin, because there's no one complexion that is more beautiful than any other. Mankind was born in Africa and populated the earth.

Therefore, every complexion of the rainbow is beautiful on its own and extraordinary when collected together.

You are a princess. Not because you are a girl, because there are many girls that will never be Queens. Not because they can't, but because either they don't know they are royal, haven't been told that they are royal, or simply choose not to acknowledge just how magnificent and significant they are. They will live their lives as fair maidens.

You are a princess. Not simply because you were born to a King and Queen. You have to know that you are loved and respected. You have to know that you are expected to show love and give respect in return. You have to love and respect yourself. Some princesses are fortunate enough to be adored, embraced, disciplined, and encouraged to be everything they dream to become. Some princesses are fortunate to have parents that instill an understanding of hard work towards success. Some princesses have parents who help to build your confidence in your abilities, so that you are self-motivated to achieve.

As a princess, you will have high expectations placed on you. You are not like others. You are different. You have a drive that can't stop and won't stop. And while it has never been formally announced to the world, it will be very obvious to all who come in contact with you. Something that stirs others to think or say, "There's something about you… that's so special, but I can't quite pin point what it is." Something in the way you speak. The way you carry yourself. The way you command respect. The way you help. The way you encourage others. The way you support others. The way you care. The way you love. Something majestic. Your uniqueness will make you stand above the crowd, as a princess should.

You are a princess.

#WhoYouComeFrom

You come from a long lineage of strong and noble queens. These women were queens, not because of anything they owned, but the knowledge, wisdom and strength they possessed. They are queens in that they were resourceful and able to make the most of what they had.

Your great grandmother was a Queen of Endurance. With nothing more than a third grade education, married at the age of 15 to someone who is twice her age, she spent her life as a servant. A servant to her husband, a servant to her five children, and a servant to those who paid her very little to be so. Her life-long career was cleaning the homes of the more affluent in the kingdom. Having the strength to leave an abusive marriage, she raised her children in shared quarters, but eventually owned her own home. She endured. She had the fortitude to continue despite fatigue, stress, trials, hardships and sickness.

My Now...

The Queen of Endurance begot the Queen of Perseverance, your grandmother. Her desire was to teach. She also had the gift of leadership. Yet she would be denied leadership opportunities in teaching, because she didn't have sufficient education. She didn't have sufficient education because she made a few bad choices. But she suffered through hardship and never gave up. On every turn, with every rejection, she pressed forward. She was determined to have the career of her dreams. She had very few options, therefore she made sacrifices for herself and her children, that she raised alone. Many times she trusted those she thought could support her, most of them eventually robbed her of the little she had. She still didn't give up. She learned to trust herself, her abilities, and her plan. She was steady and persistent on her course. Despite the difficulties and discouragement, she stayed the course reach her career dream.

The endurance and perseverance was passed down to your mother, the Queen of Audacity. She thinks highly of herself and her abilities. She believes that there's nothing that she can't accomplish. Like the Queens before her, she married young and had a child. She was told that she'd never recover from these decisions. She was told that she'd forever be indebted to the kingdom. But those who told her these things didn't know her lineage. They didn't know that the Queens before her endured and persevered much worse fates. She knew. She saw it. She was indirectly mentored by her fore-mothers. She had the audacity to attempt feats that they would never have considered.

...for the Future Woman

She had the confidence to set goals that she'd never seen achieved. She paid close attention to the failures and successes of others to build upon them. At times, she was afraid, but she never showed it. She was passive-aggressive, yet bold. She knew that she had more options than the queens before her and she aimed to exercise them all. She had a plan and if it didn't work, she developed a new plan. She climbed to the top of every organization she joined and was often recognized and rewarded for her successes. She started her own businesses—yes, more than one—and again, was publicly recognized for her successes. Then she developed programs to train others to plan and succeed. She was insatiable and always wanted and worked for more. She was audacious.

You have in your blood the endurance, perseverance, and audacity of your Queens.

#WhoYouBecome

What of *your* Queendom? You, my dear princess, are in line to become the Queen of Purpose. As the Queen of Purpose, you'll have far less challenges or hardships because the Queens before you paved the way. As the Queen of Purpose, you have been bequeathed with identifying why you were put on earth and how the world will benefit from your existence.

Beware of the maidens who will be jealous of your royalty. They will criticize everything about you. They will seek to publicly highlight any flaws; damage your reputation; and do anything to darken the light that surrounds you.

But don't let it bother you because you are a daughter of mighty Queens. Know your worth. Know that no maiden holds your fate in their hands and therefore can never darken your light. Other maidens will want to be around you in order to shine in your light. They want to know your secrets. They want to know why and how you stand tall. They want to walk like you. They want to talk like you. But they can't replicate you, because you are uniquely YOU.

Beware of misery... *it* loves company. Maidens will use *it* to make you think you're missing out. *It* will encourage you to party with pity. *It* will pressure you to miss your calling, forget your purpose, and throw you off your resolve.

As a daughter of a strong King, you've been taught how to be treated... by the way he cared for you and through the love he displayed for his Queen. He made sure that you know your worth. He is preparing you for your Prince. A genuine prince will recognize your worth immediately. And if he's a true and worthy suitor, he will usher you closer to your purpose and never pull you away from it. Understand you're your Prince may not show up on a white horse and he may not appear royal or charming. But because he too is royalty, he *too* has been prepared for you. You will recognize him by how he treats and how he sincerely makes you feel. He knows your worth and he'll be more than willing to wait.

While you wait for your Prince, Dragons will pursue you. They will try to seduce you with charm to get you to step off the path to your throne. If they aren't success, they'll try to somehow claim a piece of your royalty. Some will try to overpower you to take advantage of your royalty. When you can't be broken, they will use their strength to harm you physically or use wit and knowledge of your weaknesses to harm you mentally. But your Prince will only want to win your heart, not your body or your mind. He will want to keep you on a pedestal and treat you with the utmost respect.

#URRoyalty

You are royalty. You don't have much, but you appreciate what you've been given. And you look forward to working to earn your own. You are smart. You yearn for knowledge and seek to apply what you learn. You are brave. You've been warned of the barriers and obstacles that may come your way, but you're ready for the challenge. You believe in yourself and you act on it. And you aren't too proud to ask for help. You know who you are. You know who you come from. And you know who you will become.

You will become the Queen of Purpose. You will make a difference in this world and the lives that you touch.

My Now...

Jonathan Oliver

Jonathan Oliver is a dynamic speaker and seminar developer whose mission is to create a world of truth, love, and faith. He currently travels speaking to students of all ages about character development and leadership skills. He has been blessed with the opportunity to speak to over 3 million people.

He is the founder of Higher Enlightenment, which is a firm that provides spiritual and intelligent insight to others with the goal of helping them to believe in themselves and reach beyond their fears. He has completed his first book entitled Impersonations, co-author 3 books My Now My Vision My Plan, My Now for the Entrepreneur, My Now for the Student Leader, and is currently working on his second book where he shares how he lives and learns being dyslexic. His future endeavors include life coaching and being intimately involved in helping others fulfill their dreams.

Jonathan is an experienced speaker who has worked with companies including Toastmasters, Making it Count, Rachel's Challenge, and Moovin4Ward. He has been named a top presenter for middle school and high school assemblies. He was part of a four time division III collegiate football championship at Hardin Simmons University. He earned a Bachelor's degree in Behavioral Science with a minor in Biology. He strives to live the message that "Life is what you are born with, living is what you do with it."

...for the Future Woman

Journey

Jonathan Oliver

Before my daughter Journey was born, while she was still a tiny blueberry in my wife's womb, we began to pray every night a simple prayer: "God, please let Journey come to know Jesus at a very young age. Bless her to walk with Jesus her entire life, and when the time comes bless her to marry a God-fearing man that is growing in Your Word daily." Even now after her birth and as she continues to grow, this is our daily prayer for our daughter Journey.

Over the next couple of pages none of the information that I'm going to share is 100% my original ideas. In fact, the reason my wife and I started praying so soon for Journey is because my pastor told me that is what he and his wife did for their two children. Now they are praying for their grandchildren. Other than the book you are currently holding in your hand and reading now, I strongly suggest two other books. The first book is entitled *"Shepherding a Child's Heart"* by Tedd Trip. And since I'm raising a daughter, the second is entitled *"Strong Fathers, Strong Daughters"* by Meg Meeker, M.D. These are two excellent resources to add to your tool box when it comes to being a parent.

My Now...

While doing a bible study several months ago on the books of first and second Thessalonians, we read over 1Thessalonians 2:11-12, "For you know that we dealt with each of you as a father deals with his on children, <u>encouraging, comforting</u>, and <u>urging</u> you to live lives worthy of God, who calls you into his kingdom and glory." When everything I do is broken down to it's core foundation, my job is to encourage, comfort, and urge my daughter Journey to live a life that's going to bring glory to the name of God before the name Oliver. I'm in the unique role of being a stay at home day. This allows me to have more than just a "get in where I fit in role" in Journey's development. Within weeks after learning I was going to be a dad, I had the opportunity to attend a men's retreat. I sat in on a workshop called "Raising Young Children" and this is some of the information I was so blessed to receive.

One concept discussed Quality VS Quantity Time. This is a cultural concept, not a biblical one. Spending quality and quantity of time with Journey is not the goal: it is only the means to achieve my goal. The quality and quantity of trust is my goal.

Another concept was the Top 10 List for a father:

10. A father must cultivate a sense of family <u>identity</u>. This mean I should view my family as a team. If we have another child, remind them that they are to be best friends. We must operate as a family unit. If Dad is excited and encouraged about

the family, Journey will feel the same way. If Dad is on board, the kids will be on board. Journey will know when I am being a hypocrite.

9. A father must give his children the freedom to fail. Journey needs to have the confidence that I view her failures as first steps to success. Failure with effort is acceptable; failure without effort is not. Let them know I have failed in the past and I can share their feelings of hurt and disappointment.

8. A father must be the encourager of the family. We must encourage our children when they do something right. Take encouragement seriously; what may not be a big deal to me is a huge deal to her. Sign birthday and Christmas cards.

7. A father must guard his tongue and tone and measure his response against the excitement on his child's face. How I respond to Journey exciting news will heighten her joy or take it away. If I consistently extinguish Journey's joy, her sense of security will be violated and she will cease sharing her joy with me.

6. A father must routinely embrace his children. A gentle hand, a tender hug, a pat on the back, and a goodnight kiss all communicate intimacy in a family relationship.

Failure to communicate through touch creates a void in Journey that will be filled by anyone willing to give her that

My Now...

attention. Age and gender are not a factor and they are never too old.

5. A father must build this relationship of trust on <u>God's Word</u> not on human wisdom. Understanding God's divine plan of salvation is the start. From salvation comes sanctification, which is the divine empowerment to minister to my family. It's easy to be a parent. It's hard to be a good parent.

4. A father must <u>communicate</u> with his children. Make sure it's a dialogue not a monologue. Make a habit of talking with Journey all the time, not just when something goes wrong. Be an active listener and respect Journey's feelings. Tuck her in bed at night. Ask questions.

3. A father must keep his <u>promise</u>. I need to remember that Journey will remember what I say. Be characterized by doing what you say and you will not need to be concerned on rare occasions when something unexpected comes up.

2. A father must <u>lead</u> his children. God has delegated to me to be an authority in Journey's life. When I direct, correct, or discipline Journey, I am not acting out of my own will, but I am acting on behalf of God. Children become wise decision makers by observing parents modeling and instructing wise direction and decision making on their behalf.

...for the Future Woman

1. A father must regularly demonstrate love to his wife. Children thrive on the demonstration of love between parents. Spend time communicating with my bride while Journey is present.

I understand that this is the greatest opportunity, blessing, responsibility, duty, job, career, and honor to be a father to my daughter Journey. It all starts with me being a loving husband to her mother and my bride. Five years from now I will be the exact person I am now, the only difference will be the books I have read and the people I have drawn close to.

Books by Moovin4ward Publishing

My Now for the Future Man
Motivation and Preparation for
Moving into Manhood

By Moovin4ward Male Authors

My Now for the Student Leader
Motivation to Develop and Improve
Leadership Skills

By Moovin4ward Authors

My Now for the Single Parent
Motivation to Be The Best Parent
Regardless of Marital Status

By Moovin4ward Authors

...for the Future Woman

My Now for the College Grad:
Motivation to Succeed After College

By Moovin4ward Authors

My Now for the Entrepreneur:
Motivation to Start Your Own Business

By Moovin4ward Authors

My Vision, My Plan, MY NOW:
Motivation You Need to Take the
Action You Want

By Moovin4ward Authors

My Now…

Mapping Your Journey to Success: Six Strategies for Personal Success

By Sharon A. Myers & Mark W. Wiggins

To book a certified Moovin4ward author to speak at an event email speakers@moovin4ward.com

To purchase Moovin4ward books in bulk (20+) at discounted rates, email books@moovin4ward.com.

www.Moovin4ward.com or www.MyNowBooks.com.

www.ingramcontent.com/pod-product-compliance
Lightning Source LLC
Chambersburg PA
CBHW060144100426
42744CB00007B/896